When *Your Lead, Partner* appeared in 1964 it was an instant success. For the first time on this side of the Atlantic, two well-known British bridge authors had devoted a whole book to the vitally important matter of the opening lead, a card which can make or mar declarer's chances of success. Since then the book has been kept constantly up to date for each reprint. Study this book, with its invaluable text, quizzes and table of standard leads, and you cannot fail to get your opening leads onto the right lines – those most dangerous for your opponents.

Ben Cohen, the international player and pioneer with Terence Reese of the Acol system, died in 1971. Rhoda Lederer achieved her reputation as a bridge writer under the name of Rhoda Barrow. Co-author with Ben Cohen of a number of books on the Acol system, she has now branched out on her own, as well as producing two books in conjunction with the famous Swedish bridge player and writer, Eric Jannersten. She is also a widely experienced teacher and lecturer, and writes for a national daily, for *Bridge Magazine* and various weekly papers.

YOUR LEAD, PARTNER

Other books on bridge:

Your Lead, Partner

BEN COHEN and RHODA LEDERER

*Fully revised and brought up to date
by Rhoda Lederer*

London
UNWIN PAPERBACKS
Boston   Sydney

First published in Great Britain by George Allen & Unwin 1964
Second edition 1969
Third edition 1974
Reprinted 1976
First published as a fourth edition in Unwin Paperbacks 1979
Fifth edition 1984

UNWIN® PAPERBACKS
40 Museum Street, London WC1A 1LU

© George Allen & Unwin (Publishers) Ltd 1964, 1969, 1974, 1979, 1983

ISBN 0 04 793064 0

Printed in Great Britain by
Hazell Watson & Viney Ltd, Aylesbury, Bucks

PREFACE

The defender's opening lead can be just about the most important card in any particular deal, as it so often makes or mars declarer's chances of succeeding in his contract. You only have to think of the number of times you have heard "Sorry, partner, perhaps I should have led . . . ." or "Partner, if only you'd led . . . ." to realise the vital importance of the choice of the right card.

The correct choice, even at this early stage of the hand, will often be a simple matter. The obvious card to lead in an unbid suit or one bid by yourself or your partner will stand out a mile. Alternatively you may have to reduce the situation, by a process of elimination, to the least of evils, or even make a desperation lead when nothing but a lucky shot or the taking of declarer by surprise and misleading him can do any good to an otherwise hopeless situation.

It's easy enough to understand and to learn the table of standard leads and so, when fortunate enough to hold one of the given combinations in the right circumstances, to lead the right card of the requisite suit, and it's equally simple to learn by rote the correct card to play when leading your own or partner's bid suit. Where the difficulty arises, especially for those without a great deal of experience, is when none of the standard conditions exists, and you have to decide for yourself, with no help other than anything you may have learned during the auction, which of your thirteen cards is likely to produce the best result for your side—which may well boil down to which one is likely to do the least harm!

This latter position crops up more frequently than you may suppose. When your problem is a choice between two evils you may be able to solve it by making a "passive" lead as opposed to an attacking one. For instance, as you will learn on page 43, it is often dangerous to lead away from an unsupported honour such as a king, so if your hand contains three unsupported kings and you know of no specific reason to avoid leading the fourth suit, your choice is narrowed down for you, and you just lead the suit that doesn't contain a king. If, however, you were faced with *four* unsupported kings, you can do nothing but lead away from one of them, and your choice will have to fall on whichever suit you think least likely of the four to do harm to your side.

The rules governing the choice of opening lead are framed to help you, bearing in mind the need to give information to your partner, to protect your own holdings, and to hit declarer where it may hurt most. But such rules are not Laws of the Medes and Persians, and must be taken as generalisations. As your skill and experience increase, so will your ability to judge when they can best be broken. Never lead away from an unsupported king—never underlead an ace against a suit contract—these and many like them are good and sensible rules which you will certainly find it expedient to break at times.

The table of standard leads is set out on p. 78. It has, of course, been reproduced many times before, but it is an essential part of any book on this aspect of the game. As you will learn in Chapter 1, even these are subject to variation, and while the different methods of standard leads have their respective attractions, no particular one is overwhelmingly superior. You will have to make your own choice between them.

In the coming pages you will find a number of bidding sequences following which you will have to decide on your opening lead. These sequences are all based on standard Acol, which is the system used by the vast majority of players in this country. If you find yourself competing against one of the artificial systems, or even merely some of the innumerable conventions now in vogue, it will be up to you to make sure you know what is going on and to see that you get your full share of the inferences available which may affect your opening lead. Against Acol players, for example, a non-vulnerable 1 N.T. opening bid will show 12-14 honour points and probably —though this is not a promise—no five-card suit. A Vienna player's 1 N.T. opening shows a very powerful hand with no reference whatsoever to the distribution or any particular suit, and a Neopolitan 1 N.T. shows 13-16 points with at least a four-card club suit, possibly longer.

Even Acol players use a number of conventional bids, and several of the simpler examples come to mind. If, for instance, on the way up to a slam contract against you, your partner doubles an opponent's cue bid, he would clearly be asking for a lead of that suit. If in response to an Acol 1 N.T. his partner makes the fit-finding bid of 2♣, which your partner doubles, he would be asking for a club lead. (This 2♣ response, by the way, is widely though erroneously attributed to Stayman though it was, in fact, invented and developed by the British players Ewart Kempson and Jack Marx.) As a final example, if, during the auction, your partner has put in an "Unusual No Trump" bid, you will know in which suits he was showing interest and can lead accordingly.

There are, of course, endless other examples one could cite, but the point we are making is that you must at all times be wide awake.

Don't be put off too easily from your natural lead by an opponent's artificial bid. If your partner has offered a suggestion, either by way of a natural intervening bid or one you judge to be artificial, such as the Unusual No Trump, grasp the help given to you. Always stop to think. Work out the possible, if not the probable, holdings of the other three players, and then apply any positive knowledge you have gained as well as your judgement, to making the best available lead in the circumstances known to you, and this will require both deduction and logic. For the rest, you may often have to resort to sheer inspiration!

*   *   *

When I first revised this book in 1969, I acknowledged with thanks permission from "Bridge Magazine" to quote from its pages, and also the help given by my old friend Mervyn Morgan, then of New Zealand and now of Kenya. Both these acknowledgements stand, as none of the items concerned have been cut.

Roman Leads, which were pretty new in this country in 1969, are now in fairly general use, and have since been joined by Journalist and 'Attitude' leads, details of which you will find set out briefly in Chapter 1.

The main revisions in this new edition, though, concern the modern practice, which has now become "standard", of leading the ace instead of the king from A-K combinations, the lead of the king now having joined the ranks of top-of-a-sequence leads. Example hands, the quiz questions, and the table of standard leads have all been amended so as to be in keeping.

I hope you will find this new revised edition of *Your Lead, Partner* even more helpful than the previous one.

R. L.
1983

CONTENTS

CHAPTER 1

General Rules for "Blind" Leads

A "BLIND" opening lead, that is, one made when you have no obvious choice dictated by partner's bidding, is completely different according to whether you are defending a suit or a no-trump contract. In either case, though, there are accepted leads from certain specific holdings, so before we go into the reasoning which helps to dictate your choice of lead on any particular hand, we will deal with the general rules for "blind" leads.

a.) **Standard Leads:** A standard lead, that is, the lead of a particular card from a particular holding, is used when the opening lead is to be in a suit *not* bid by the leader's partner. The table of these standard leads is set out on p. 78, and you will quickly come to know it by heart though, as you will see later, you will by no means automatically choose one of them even if your hand contains them—there may be a quite different and better lead indicated.

Over the years, as any woman knows, fashions change. Skirts shoot up and down—or virtually vanish, and men have their hair "styled", permed and coloured. So why should bridge stand still in a world of change? Indeed, it hasn't done so. For decades it was "standard" to lead the king from a suit headed by either the A-K or K-Q against a trump suit contract. Nowadays this fashion has changed, and the "standard" lead from a suit headed by the A-K-x or more, or the A-K-Q, is the ace. From the K-Q or more you lead the king. Thus right from the start your partner is in little doubt about your honour holding.

One of the reasons for this development is that it is so vitally important for the defending partnership to know as quickly as possible what each of them holds, so that they can plan the defence. Another reason is that the lead of the ace from A-K combinations foils any attempt by declarer to catch the defenders in a "Bath Coup". This is the hold-up by declarer of the ace when the king is led, which may tempt the defence to continue the suit to declarer's

```
                N.
               ♡ 9 8 4
                W.           E. (you)
           ♡ K Q 10 6 2   ♡ 7 5
                S.
               ♡ A J 3
```

advantage. Here, for instance, if West leads the ♡K against a spade contract, you will know that it is useless to start an encouraging peter with the ♡7, in the hope that West has the ♡A too. If you do, and South drops his ♡3, the next heart lead from West will be in the free gifts department for South. On the other hand, if the situation is as in this

```
                N.
               ♡ 9 8 4
            W.              E. (you)
          ♡ K led          ♡ J 7 5
                S.
                ?
```

second diagram, you know that West has the ♡Q and that you can safely peter with the ♡7, as your ♡J will back him up and you will possibly force declarer to use up a much needed trump if he wants to win the third heart trick. You will also know from the start that declarer has the ♡A.

There are still pockets of resistance to change, so don't be too surprised if you meet people who have not yet graduated to leading the ace from A-K combinations.

Even though the method just described is now standard, there are two exceptions to it, the first being in defence of a trump contract, when the A-K holding is a doubleton. If your customary lead is the ace from A-K-x, from A-K-doubleton you lead the king followed by the ace, telling partner that you can ruff the third round of the suit if given the chance. Similarly, of course, if you still prefer to lead the king from A-K-x, then with a doubleton you would lead the ace followed by the king, giving the same information. The other exception is a special conventional lead of the ace in the defence of a no trump contract, which you will find set out in detail in Chapter 2.

As the lead of the ace from three-card or longer holdings which include the king or king and queen are regarded as standard nowadays, the examples in this book are based on this method and are, you will find, in line with the table on page 78.

b.) **Roman Leads:** There is another system of opening leads about which you should know, particularly as this has been licensed by the English Bridge Union for use in any competitions and tournaments run under its auspices. These will concern you if you decide to use them yourself, or if you want to avoid being misled if they are used against you.

Roman Leads are used only on the initial lead against a suit contract, and in a suit which partner has not bid. With two honours in sequence the *lower* of the two is led, except when the holding is a doubleton, when the higher is played first. Thus from K-Q-doubleton the king is led, and from K-Q-x, the queen. With three honours in sequence, the middle card followed by the lower is led, thus from A-K-Q the king followed by the queen, or from K-Q-J the queen followed by the knave. When leading from an interior sequence, the second-highest of touching cards (not the highest as in standard leads) is led, so from K-J-10 the ten is led, and from K-10-9, the nine. Apart from this initial lead, that is, either later in the hand or if leading partner's bid suit, the highest of touching honours is led.

Just for the record, this principle of leading the second-highest of touching honours was devised in America the best part of forty years ago by Sydney Rusinow. Until quite recently these Roman— or Rusinow—Leads were barred, both by the English Bridge Union and the American Contract Bridge League. Now, however, they are perfectly "legal" and are used by many of the leading experts of our day, so any would-be tournament player should at least understand them. After all, if a standard lead gives information to partner, it also gives it to declarer, who is entitled by the laws of the game to a full understanding of any partnership agreements. Thus if declarer is only aware of the meaning of *standard* leads and expects the lead of a queen to deny the holding of the king, he will be at a great disadvantage if his opponents are using Roman leads, when the queen will promise the king. His whole play may be upset by placing the errant king in the wrong defender's hand!

c.) **Journalist Leads:** Another recruit to join the list of permitted systems of leads is this. I can't, myself, see that it has many advantages, but at least if it is explained to you, you will know what is happening if it is used against you.

When making a lead in a suit not bid by partner:

i) Against Suit contracts lead:
    a) The lower or lowest of touching honours.
    b) Third highest from an even number of cards in the suit.
    c) Lowest from an odd number of cards in the suit.

ii) Against No-Trump contracts lead:
    a) No fourth best leads.
    b) 2, 3, 4 or 5 shows interest in the suit and demands its return by partner at the first opportunity.
    c) 6, 7, 8 or 9 is passive, showing little interest in the suit.
    d) The 10 guarantees another honour higher than the knave.
    e) The knave guarantees a higher honour in that suit, the queen guarantees the king and the king guarantees the ace.
    f) The ace demands unblock by partner.

d.) **Attitude Leads:** Another new idea is, instead of a fourth best, to indicate your "attitude" towards your lead. The lower the pips of the card led against a no-trump contract, the stronger the indication that the lead should be returned and, conversely, the higher the pips, the less likely are you to want the suit returned. Thus you express your "attitude" towards the suit rather than giving any sort of count on it.

*   *   *

In the defence of a no-trump contract, except when you are the lucky possessor of a strong suit headed by high honours, you will usually be leading a low card from your longest suit in an attempt to knock out declarer's stoppers before he, in turn, knocks out your possible entries. Unless you hold one of the combinations shown for leads against no-trump contracts in the table on p. 78 you will usually lead the fourth best of your longest suit. Why, though, the fourth best? Many beginners find this hard to understand, so we will spare a little time for an explanation.

e.) **The Rule of Eleven:** If your partner leads, for example, the ♡7, which you guess to be the fourth best of his longest suit, you know that the 8, 9, 10, J, Q, K and A are around somewhere. That is a total of seven cards *above* the ♡7. In other words, the eighth card from the top of the suit has been led and the missing seven remain to be located. Your partner, however, if he has led his fourth best, has three of these missing cards, leaving only four to be located. This is the arithmetical result of deducting 7, the pip number of the card led, from the formula figure of eleven, hence the Rule of Eleven.

For those of you who want to know how the formula figure of eleven is reached, here is a brief explanation, though you may find it a little difficult to follow. So you can skip the rest of this paragraph if your only interest is in *how* it works, not why. We have already said that if West leads a 7, his fourth best, the 8, 9, 10, J, Q, K and A, seven cards, remain to be located. Numbering from 8 upwards instead of naming the honour cards, we arrive at the fact that 8, 9, 10, 11, 12, 13 and 14 remain to be located. Of these West has three, so knock off the last three from your mental list, leaving yourself with the eighth, ninth, tenth and *eleventh,* four cards, or 7, the card led, deducted from 11. So it goes on down the scale, if a 6 is led, 6 from 11 = 5, to be located.

It is frequently possible by the use of this rule to place the missing cards accurately. For example, the ♠6 is led in this diagram. Deduct 6 from 11=5, so there are five spades higher than the ♠6 to be located, and these will be divided between dummy, your own hand, and declarer's. Dummy has three of the five and you have two, which accounts for all of them. Declarer, therefore, has *no* spade higher than the ♠6. So if dummy's ♠7 is played,

N.
♠ K J 7

W.   E. (you)
♠6 led   ♠ Q 9 3

S.
♠ ?

you are safe to play your ♠9, to win the trick. If dummy's ♠J is played you, of course, play the ♠Q which is also sure to win the trick for the simple reason that you know West started with three spades higher than the ♠6 and by a process of deduction can also see that these must be the ♠A-10-8. How many he holds *below* the ♠6 remains to be seen, and will develop later in the play of the hand.

N.
♡ 6 5 3

W.   E. (you)
♡4 led   ♡ K 9

S.
♡ ?

In this next diagram you deduct 4, the pip number of the card led, from 11, and discover that seven cards higher than the ♡4 remain to be located. Dummy and you both have two of them, so declarer must have three. You go up with your ♡K and declarer plays the ♡2. Now it is evident that West has led from a four-card suit only—the ♡2 and ♡3 are both visible, and there isn't another heart lower than the ♡4, which we know to be his fourth best, that he can hold. If declarer plays the ♡7 at trick 1, it is logical to assume that he hasn't got the ♡2 and that, therefore, West has it, and has led from a five-card suit.

There are occasions when the application of the Rule of Eleven gives little or no helpful information but, as you can see, there are others on which it will reveal not only the location of the missing cards, but the length of the suit that has been led. Here's another

N.
♡ K 10 5 4

W.   E. (you)
♡7 led   ♡ A Q 9 6 2

S.
♡ ?

example, which brings out a different point. Deducting 7 from 11 we arrive at the fact that, if West has led his fourth highest heart, there are four higher than the ♡7 to be located. But dummy has two and you three, a total of five. This can only mean that West has *not* led a fourth-best, so he has probably led from a worthless short suit.

Note, by the way, that declarer too can often apply the Rule of Eleven, to discover something about the missing cards held by *East*.

```
        N.
        ♡ Q 10 7

W.              E.
♡4 led          ♡ ?

        S.
        ♡ A 6 5
```

In this diagram, South deducts 4 from 11 and finds that there are seven cards outstanding higher than the ♡4. He can see six of these, so East has only one. When dummy's ♡7 is played East produces the ♡K. As this must be East's only high heart the rest of the suit is marked, and it is perfectly safe to win with the ♡A and, later, finesse the ♡10 in the knowledge that West must hold the ♡J. So occasionally, when you are certain that precise knowledge is more likely to help declarer than your partner, it may pay dividends to make a completely false lead which cannot be read correctly by anyone!

f.) **The Rule of Twelve:** Another recent innovation is the lead of the *third* best card of your longest suit, not the fourth best as set out above. The mechanics of this are exactly as set out for the Rule of Eleven except that, this time, you deduct the pips of the card led from twelve instead of eleven.

If you feel that all this may be a trifle confusing, don't worry— stick to the good old fourth best until you feel like trying it. At least you will know that this new idea is now quite widely in use and will have a chance, not only to understand it if it is used against you, but to decide whether to adopt it yourself.

It is claimed that the most valuable feature of the third best lead is that it reduces the number of higher unknown cards. In this

```
        N.
        ♡ J 9 3

W.                      E.
♡ Q 8 7 4 2    ♡ K 10 5

        S.
        ♡ A 6
```

diagram, for example, a lead of the ♡4, West's fourth best, will show East that declarer has two hearts higher than the ♡4. Leading the third best ♡7 reduces this to one.

Leads from three-card holdings headed by an honour will come more into the realms of probability when the lead is no longer "blind", that is to say, when suits have been shown, but since part of the argument in favour of third best leads is involved,

```
        N.
        ♡ 10 5 3

W.              E.
♡ K 7 4         ♡ A J 9 8

        S.
        ?
```

we may as well cover it now. If, for instance, for strategic reasons, West thinks that a heart lead is indicated against South's no-trump contract, what East will expect to be a fourth best when West leads the ♡4 will make East think that declarer may hold either the ♡Q-J-2 or the ♡K-Q-2, and that a heart continuation may cost the defence a "tempo". If using third best leads it becomes quite clear that South has only one stop, the king, queen, or knave. In the next diagram, if West is known to be leading third best East can, if his ♡J holds, safely underlead the ♡A at trick 2. If using fourth best leads, he must guess.

N.
♡ Q 5 3

W.   E.
♡ K 7 4   ♡ A J 9 8

S.
♡ 10 6 2

There is one instance when a third best lead can give an inferior picture, and that is when declarer holds no card higher than the one led and that need not concern you very deeply as learners.

It would be tedious if, throughout the rest of this book, whenever the question of a fourth or a third best lead crops up, we were to refer you to the fact that there is the alternative. From now on, then, we shall speak of what is still, after all, the standard method of fourth best, just as we shall speak of leading the ace from ace-king combinations.

g.) **Doubleton Leads:** There is only one accepted way of leading from a worthless doubleton holding, and that is the higher card followed by the lower, that is to say, the 9 from 9-6 or the 8 from 8-3. It is very, very seldom advisable, and that only as a measure of desperation, to lead the honour from K-x or Q-x, as neither of these holdings can be considered worthless and may well produce a trick if led through to your hand later. Never lead low from A-x against a suit contract—if you must lead the suit, lead the ace. It must, however, be admitted that if you can judge the moment correctly and are willing to take the chance that it will turn out to be a costly mistake, it can pay dividends to lead the king from K-x, as if partner turns out to have the ace, you may get in a devastating ruff on the third round. The ace from A-x can also be successful if partner turns out to have the king, in addition to which this lead at least has the merit of risking less than the king lead.

The exception to this rule of leading the top of a doubleton was explained on p. 14, when your holding is A-K doubleton. In general, however, we are considering leads from a worthless doubleton, the higher card first, inevitably to be followed on the second round of the suit by the lower.

h.) **Tripleton Leads:** In this context we are considering only a *worthless* tripleton, so that the first point is that a 9 can never be considered worthless, as it has quite a high trick-taking potential or promotion-value. So an opening lead even from three meagre cards, if headed by the 9, should be avoided if possible. The exception to this is, of course, if you happen to hold 9-8-7 in sequence.

There are three ways of leading from a worthless tripleton, so let us first dispose of the completely fallacious so-called "modern" method of leading the lowest card first. One example should suffice to show how very misleading this can be to your partner, who will almost certainly think you are leading low from three or more to an honour.

♠ J 6 4
♡ A 7 6 3
◇ 9 3
♣ A K 6 4

♠ 3   ♠ A Q 10 8 7 2
♡ 9 8 4 2   ♡ Q J 10
◇ 8 7 2   ◇ 4
♣ J 9 5 3 2   ♣ Q 10 7

♠ K 9 5
♡ K 5
◇ A K Q J 10 6 5
♣ 8

From a team of four match, both South players became declarer in 6◇, and both West players led the singleton ♠3. In the open room East was in no doubt—he went up with the ♠A and returned a second spade for West to ruff before declarer even got off the ground.

In the closed room the East-West defenders were using low from three worthless cards and declarer was quick to recognise the danger as well as his possible chance to avert it—he smoothly dropped the ♠K on East's ♠A. This risked a two-trick defeat, but this was nothing compared with his chance of gain. As he had hoped, East did not dare to lead a second spade, fearing to set up dummy's knave. East switched to a heart and South was able to set up a squeeze to make his contract. You will note that, even had declarer in the open room dropped his ♠K, East would not have been deceived, as he would *know* that West would not have led low from ♠9-5-3.

So our advice to you is to ignore this method and take your pick from the other two.

To take the older, traditional one first, you lead the *top* card, which is known as "top of nothing", and follow this with the *middle* card of the three. That is to say, you lead the card in heavy type in any of these examples, and follow it with the next lower, not the lowest of the three:

8 6 2:   **7** 5 3:   **6** 4 2:   **5** 3 2:

If you lead a worthless-looking card followed by a lower one, as in the previous section, partner is liable to take this for a doubleton and try to give you a ruff on the third round of the suit. How, then, is he to distinguish a genuine doubleton from a "top of nothing"? The answer is that you may be able to make this more clear to him by playing your middle card next—the 6 in the first example, the

5 in the second, and so on. Your partner who, it is to be hoped, has been watching the fall of the cards, will see that, in the first instance the 2 has not yet appeared, and in the second, the 3 is still not accounted for. From this it is only a short step to deducing that the missing card is still in your hand and that, therefore, you have led from the top of three cards and not from a doubleton, and will *not* be able to ruff the third round. If your partner doesn't see or, having seen, make the necessary deduction, we leave it to you what to do about him!

The other accepted method is familiarly known as MUD— Middle Up and Down. This method, though it has been in use for many years, has now received a good deal of publicity and is gaining steadily in popularity.

Using MUD on the same example holdings, lead the 6 followed by the 8 in the first, the 5 followed by the 7 in the second, and so on. Thus there is no possible chance that partner will mistake the holding for a doubleton. This is a doubt which, using the previous method, can often be fostered by judicious false-carding from declarer, even though you are careful to play the middle card to the second trick. Leading the middle first and following it with the higher, the only possible doubt would be whether it were a fourth best from a suit headed by an honour. In this connection, however, as you will see in Chapter 2, we have been at some pains to eliminate the habit of leading low from an unsupported honour.

On balance we would very definitely recommend MUD leads in defence of a suit contract and the old "top of nothing", at any rate for learners, in defence of no-trump contracts. But always remember that a holding headed by an honour, even the 10, does *not* qualify for a MUD lead, and nor must you *ever* make a MUD lead from any three cards of partner's bid suit (see p. 52).

* * *

Here, then, you have the general rules—whether you choose "Attitude", "Standard", "Roman" or "Journalist", third- or fourth-best, MUD or "top of nothing". But many other factors have to be taken into account when making your choice, so now let us go on from the general to the particular.

CHAPTER 2

Leads against No Trump Contracts

THERE'S all the difference in the world in the choice of opening lead against a no-trump and against a trump contract. In the former, with which we shall concern ourselves now, the defence will frequently be a battle of "tempos", that is, a race to establish winners in a long suit or suits before essential entry cards are knocked out. Declarer will be trying to set up his own winners and, in the process, to remove the defenders' entry cards and cut their communications before their established cards become a menace. At the same time the defenders will be trying to conserve their entries so that, once established, they will be able to enjoy the fruits of their labours. So in the case of the defence to no-trump contracts—with a few exceptions which we shall come to later— the defenders will not be playing off, or "cashing", their high card tricks, but will be conserving them as entries later in the play.

1). LEADS AGAINST SIMPLE NO-TRUMP CONTRACTS

a.) **No Trump Opening & Direct Raise:** Declarer's no-trump contract may have been reached in a variety of ways. What we shall term "simple" no-trump contracts are those which have been bid by way of a no-trump opening and a direct raise in no-trumps, 1 N.T.—3 N.T., or perhaps 1 N.T.—2 N.T.—3 N.T., with no suit having been shown on the way. As the opening leader you will have no inhibitions against leading any particular suit, in which case a very normal choice will be the fourth-best of your longest suit (or third-best if that is your chosen method) as described in Chapter 1. If you are lucky enough to find partner with some support for you in it, or even if you have a possible entry in your own hand, it is important to get the matter of clearing the suit under way.

It is equally important, however, not to make life easier than you can help for declarer. Hands bid as above are likely to be made up of high cards and tenaces without long suits. In such cases, unless you can see some future from attacking in a long suit, it is generally wiser to play a passive role. Don't give declarer a

N.
♠ A 9 2

W. (you)   E.
♠ Q 7 6 4   ♠ 10 5 3

S.
♠ K J 8

"free" trick by leading away from a single unsupported honour. Hold on to such suits in the hope that declarer will have to take a finesse into your hand. Here, for example, the lead of a small spade gives South three certain tricks in this suit whereas, left to himself, he may well finesse the knave into your hand. He may, of course, be able to avoid this by an end-play, but at least make him work for his living!

b.) **Sequence Leads:** The best and safest lead, if you are lucky enough to have such a holding, will generally be from the top of a sequence, which is not likely to give anything away. If you haven't got a sequence, or any other apparently helpful lead, then choose the suit which most nearly constitutes a sequence.

♠ J 10 9 6
♡ K J 7 4
◇ 8 4 3
♣ 7 2

Lead the ♠J from this hand. It is far wiser than the ♡4 which stands an excellent chance of being straight in declarer's ♡A-Q or perhaps, just as bad, the ♡A on the table and the ♡Q in his own hand. The ♠J lead cannot be worse than through any honour your partner may hold, which declarer could finesse for himself in any case.

♠ 9 3
♡ Q 7 5 4
◇ Q 10 9 6
♣ 7 6 3

Here your best choice is the ◇10. If your partner has the ◇K, or ◇A, or even only the ◇J, you are on your way to setting up a couple of tricks in diamonds before your only possible entry, the ♡Q, is knocked out.

Sometimes you are faced with a direct choice between two practically equal suits both of which contain a sequence, or near-sequence. Bidding four-card major suits is normal practice, whereas it is quite usual to conceal even a five-card minor in favour of a bid in no-trumps. If, therefore, no suit bidding by your opponents has suggested a choice between spades and diamonds when you have to lead from a hand such as this, it is wiser to select the major suit, spades, than the minor, all other things being equal, on the grounds that as neither declarer nor his partner has shown even a four-card spade suit, you may well strike oil in partner's hand.

♠ Q 10 9 7
♡ 9 7 6
◇ Q 10 9 7
♣ J 3

c.) **Considering Entries:** The question of entry cards is important, and must always be taken into consideration when selecting your lead. It isn't much good setting up a long suit if you have no chance at all of getting in to make your master cards in it when you've got them established! So, for example, your best choice on this hand would be the ◇6 (fourth best), not the ♣4. Either suit needs help from your partner if it is to be established, but

♠ 9 6
♡ 4
◇ Q 9 8 6 3
♣ A 7 5 4 2

you have just as good a chance of finding him able to help with diamonds as with clubs. If you lead the diamond, you will still have the ♣A which may provide an entry to them if and when established, whereas there is far less chance that the ◇Q will provide an entry to any established clubs.

Unless you are a complete beginner you will already know that it is not always a good idea to lead away from a tenace, but this is a generalisation only, particularly in the defence of simple no-trump contracts. Be very wary about leading from such combinations as A-Q-x-x, K-J-x-x, K-Q-x-x, Q-x-x-x, or J-x-x-x. Add a fifth card to any of them, however, and they may become well worth an attacking lead in the suit. If you lead your fourth best from, for example, A-Q-x-x-x, the first lead will remove one card from declarer's hand and, if subsequently your partner gains the lead, another through from him up to your remaining A-Q-x-x may produce four winners which, added to the trick your partner has taken, leaves 3 N.T. doomed to defeat.

♠ 9 2
♡ A 8 7 3
◇ A 6
♣ Q 8 7 5 3

On this hand you may feel you have a choice between leading your four-card major or your five-card minor, but there really isn't any choice at all. Lead your ♣5. You have two entries in your red suit aces which, with any luck, will enable you to get in to run off any established clubs you may be able to set up.

What, though, would your choice of lead from a hand such as

♠ K J 8 2
♡ 9 8
◇ J 9 7 4 3
♣ Q 2

this be? Your spade honours may give you an entry if you are able to establish the diamonds, but this time you choose the ◇4, *not* because you have much hope of establishing the suit, but because you must not be tempted to lead away from your spade tenace, which will almost inevitably give declarer an extra trick.

Occasionally you will find yourself on lead against a no-trump contract when you hold a reasonable long suit which you might well establish, but you have no shred of an entry card outside it. Let's say, for example, that the bidding has gone 1♡—2◇—3NT, and now you are on lead from this hand: —

♠ K Q J 10 7
♡ 9 7 5
◇ 8 7 4
♣ 8 2

Neither hearts nor diamonds appear to have any future for your side, and even if your partner has any sort of a club suit of his own your doubleton isn't going to help him much. So you are left with your spades. You should lead the ♠K and continue leading them firmly unless you get some very positive information that a switch is indicated. The reason for this is two-fold. In the first place declarer might have bid his 3 N.T. with no more than

♠A-x and, if your partner has three spades and can win a trick in any other suit, he will be able to put you on play again. Secondly, declarer will know all about the uselessness of plugging a long suit from a hand with no side suit entry. The mere fact, therefore, that you continue to plug it, may trap him into electing to take a two-way finesse into your partner's hand rather than your own later in the play, on the assumption that you, not your partner, hold a missing honour card which may become an entry to your established spades. He may also, of course, be forced to "run for home", foregoing the chance of possible over-tricks, because of the menace of your long spades.

Apart from an occasion such as the above, never waste time or effort in trying to establish a suit of your own when you have a worthless hand and no chance of getting in again. In such cases it is better to concentrate on trying to help your partner. After all, the less you have, the more he may have, which brings us to our next item.

d.) **Short Suit Leads:** A short suit lead may be used either to get you out of trouble, that is, when you feel that any other suit you lead is likely to cost your side a trick, or when, having a worthless hand, it is safer not to encourage your partner into thinking you have a suit worth establishing. This he is generally likely to think if you lead a fourth best or what looks like a fourth best. This is a pretty

♠ 8 6 3
♡ Q 9 4 3
◇ 10 8 6 4
♣ 7 3

hopeless hand from a defensive point of view, so your most promising line of defence will be to conserve what little you have whilst praying that your partner is better off than you are! It would be better to lead the ◇4 than the ♡3, but either of these suits, if left untouched, *may* yield a trick later. The best of all, then, is to make a short suit lead.

When a short suit lead seems indicated in the defence of a no-trump contract, it is usually wiser to choose a worthless trebleton rather than a worthless doubleton, and this holds good especially if you have a possible entry in your hand. The reason for this is that if your short suit lead has the luck to strike oil in partner's hand, your third card will give you an excellent chance of getting him in again once the suit is cleared.

♠ K 9 8
♡ 8 6 4
◇ 9 7 6 5 3
♣ 8 4

In spite of your ♠K, this hand is too barren to make a fourth best diamond lead worth while—you would need to find partner with an exceptional diamond fit to have any hope of clearing it. So give up this slender chance in favour of a short suit heart lead.

For the choice of *which* heart to lead, turn back to Section (f) of Chapter 1, the "top of nothing" ♡8 or the "MUD" ♡6.

♠ J 8 6 4
♡ K J 5
◇ 10 9
♣ A Q 10 7

This hand offers no desirable lead against a simply bid no-trump contract, as clearly you would prefer spades, hearts, and clubs to be led through to you. Lead your ◇10, which your partner can't possibly mistake for anything but a short suit lead. If he has diamonds himself it will give him a start towards establishing the suit without touching any possible entry he may have. On the other hand, if he's not personally interested in diamonds he will select a switch any time he may gain the lead, and this can hardly help being to your advantage. Add a fifth club in place of, say, the ◇9, and you should lead your fourth best club without a moment's hesitation. Not only have you a good chance of establishing the suit, but you have possible entry cards to get in with once it is cleared.

♠ 10 8 6 4 2
♡ 8 6 3
◇ 9 7 4
♣ 6 5

Don't lead your fourth best spade on this hand—it would be wasted effort, as you have no possible chance of an entry to the suit later on, even if it can be established. This is a moment to try to find something to help your partner so, for the reasons set out at the end of Section (b) of this chapter, lead a heart (either "top of nothing" ♡8 or "MUD" ♡6), going for the major suit rather than the minor when both seem equally unpromising.

From the above you must not get the idea that you should never attack in a weak or weakish long suit. In these days of weak no-trump openings it is the exception rather than the rule for opener to have all four suits fully guarded, and often he will have opened 1 N.T. with no better than Q-x, J-x, or even as bad as a losing doubleton in one suit. It is also quite amazing how often such a holding turns out to be facing the same weak suit in dummy. So with a five-card suit or better headed by an honour and any possible chance of an entry, open the attack in your suit. Here, for instance,

♠ K 10 8 5 3
♡ 9 7 5
◇ A 6 4
♣ J 6

don't let your fear of giving away a spade trick outweigh your common sense. Of course a spade lead *may* give declarer a safe trick, but it *may* also cost him his contract. Suppose partner has the ♠A-x-x or the ♠Q-x-x: either holding gives you the chance of four spade tricks plus the ◇A to defeat 3 N.T.

N.
♠ J 6 2

W.   E.
♠ K 10 8 5 3   ♠ A 7

S.
♠ Q 9 4

Here, in fact, is the spade distribution as it actually was on this duplicate hand. The ♠5 was won by East's ace, the ♠7 came back to West's king, and a third spade felled declarer's queen and dummy's knave in one stroke, and declarer was unable to run his nine tricks before losing to the ◇A. Several

defenders chose the passive heart lead, and South cantered home.
e.) Which Card to Lead: Having decided which suit to lead on
any given hand, the next important point is which card to select.
We've already dealt with your choice from short suits, so now, when
it is not a simple alternative of fourth best of your longest suit, you
must turn your attention to honour combinations. Here it is possible
to help you with general rules.

From a complete sequence, if you are lucky enough to have one,
lead the top card. There's one exception to this—the lead of an
ace in the defence of a no-trump contract is best used conventionally.
Details of this are set out in Section (f) of this chapter. Meanwhile,
by a complete sequence we mean a run of at least three adjacent
cards, such as K-Q-J, Q-J-10, 10-9-8, and so on. Two touching
cards do not constitute a sequence, and if the suit in question has
to be led, it is generally better to choose the fourth best.

With a near sequence, however, such as K-Q-10-9 or J-10-8-x,
you may treat the holding as a sequence, mentally up-grading the
third card by one pip, and lead the top. These last combinations don't
make ideal leads by any means, and you should try only to fall back
on them if you can find nothing better. It is quite extraordinary how
many times, in actual practice, they can cost the defence a trick.

With the best will in the world occasions will arise when it is
impossible to think of a better line of
attack than a diamond from a suit like
this. But if the distribution happens to
be as shown in this diagram, the lead
of the ◇K will give declarer two certain
diamond tricks whereas, left to himself,
he would be very hard put to it to make
more than one. Here is the full hand

```
            N.
          ◇ J 6 3

W.                    E.
◇ K Q 10 9 7     ◇ 8 2

            S.
          ◇ A 5 4
```

from which this suit was taken. It comes from a duplicate pairs
event, where over-tricks can be worth their weight in gold.

```
          ♠ Q 10 8 6
          ♡ K J 6
          ◇ J 6 3
          ♣ 7 3 2
♠ 4 2                   ♠ A 7 5 3
♡ 7 5                   ♡ 9 8 4 3
◇ K Q 10 9 7            ◇ 8 2
♣ 10 9 8 4              ♣ Q J 6
          ♠ K J 9
          ♡ A Q 10 2
          ◇ A 5 4
          ♣ A K 5
```

The bidding had been 2 N.T. (20-22
points) from South, raised to 3 N.T.
by North, and several West players
mistakenly made the foolish "attacking" lead of the ◇K. After this
nothing could prevent South from
making 3 N.T.+2, losing only one
diamond and the ♠A. Note how
much better the defenders fared after
a passive or "waiting" lead of the
♣10! Now South can make no more
than one over-trick, but that can be

the difference between a "top" and a "bottom" at duplicate pairs, and even at rubber bridge, the extra 30 points can tip the scales towards the loss of an extra 100 points in the final reckoning.

For the leads from other combinations, turn to the table of standard leads on p. 78, but to summarise, if you hold a five-card or better suit with a reasonable chance of entry when it is cleared, lead your fourth best (or third best if that is your choice of method) unless you hold one of the combinations in the table, when select the appropriate card. With two five-card suits, unless there is a good chance of establishing one of them in one round, lead the *weaker* of the two, hoping to use any high cards in the stronger as entries. With two four-card suits lead the one least likely to give away a trick, that is, avoid leading away from a single unsupported honour or a wide-open tenace. In other words, don't risk giving away a trick unless there appears to be a chance of developing other worthwhile tricks in the suit. Make an attacking lead only when this seems to be your best chance of defeating the contract, but otherwise make a passive, or waiting lead which is unlikely to give away a trick and gives you an opportunity to find out how the land lies.

Inevitably you will make the wrong choice at times, but on balance the tactics outlined above will pay dividends.

f.) **Conventional Ace-Lead:** This is a very useful convention, and one which you would be well advised to add to your armoury. In the defence of a no-trump contract, the opening lead of an ace is a demand to partner to unblock the suit by playing his highest card on the first round, which may at the same time give you vital information about the distribution of the missing cards in it. Remember, of course, that this convention would *not* apply if partner had bid the suit, and nor will West, the holder of the suit in question be likely to have bid it because, if he had, it is hardly credible that the opposition will subsequently have settled for a contract in no-trumps. Nor would it apply in the defence to an opening pre-emptive 3 N.T. bid, or when an opening three-bid has been converted to 3 N.T., as in either of these cases it is frequently a good policy to cash an ace "to take a look". (See Section 5 on p. 39.)

Using this conventional ace lead and holding, for example, ◇ A-K-Q-10-8-7, the ace at Trick 1 requires partner to drop his highest diamond. If this happens to be the knave there is no risk whatsoever of the suit being blocked at a later stage, apart from which the leader will already know that declarer hasn't got it! If, instead of the knave, partner drops the ◇6, this places declarer with at least ◇J-9 (unless either of these can be seen in dummy). Similarly, if the ace is led from ◇ A-K-J-10-8-5, partner will drop the ◇Q if he has it, and any possible danger of the suit being blocked at round three will be eliminated. If, however, the best partner can produce is the ◇6, declarer is marked with ◇Q-9-7 (if not in dummy), when the only chance may be to wait until your partner can be put on play to lead through declarer's hand towards your tenace.

2). WHEN OPPONENTS HAVE BID A SUIT

1♡ —2NT   Very frequently your opponents will end up in a
3NT   no-trump contract after either one or both of them
                 has bid a suit on the way, and this must, of course,
1♡ —1♠   alter your tactics. Sometimes the bidding will have
2NT—3NT   been very positive, as in the first two example
                 sequences. On the other hand it may have been
1◇ —1♠   a somewhat reluctant struggle which, as in this third
2♣ —2♠   sequence, gives away the fact that, though your
2NT—3NT   opponents feel a game should be available, they
                 aren't quite sure of the best final resting place.
Again, the contract may have been reached by way of the 2♣ fit-finding bid, and any such factors can give you clues as to your best line of attack.

a.) **The Enemy's Suit:** Unless you have reason to suspect the opposition of a psychic suit bid, or you have some unusual strength in it, you should avoid attacking in a suit bid by declarer, that is, the opponent on your right, as you will be leading *up* to his hand. We'll go into this more fully presently but, meanwhile, look at

♠ Q 10 9 6 3   this hand. If the bidding has been simply 1 N.T.—
♡ A 9   3 N.T., you would not hesitate to lead a spade. You
◇ K 8 4   have an excellent five-card suit and two possible
♣ 9 7 2   entries. But suppose that 1♠ has been opened on
                 your right—which obviously you pass—and the
bidding goes 1♠—2◇—2NT—3NT. Now the last thing you must do is help declarer to extra spade tricks. If he has started with, for example, ♠A-K-J-8, a spade lead will give him three certain tricks whereas, left to himself, two will be his limit. This would be a moment for a short suit club lead.

On the other hand, leading *through* a suit bid by your left hand

♠ K 9 4   opponent, who is going to be dummy, may well get
♡ Q J 7 4   you out of trouble. You find yourself on lead from
◇ 6 5 2   this hand after the sequence 1♡—2◇—2NT—3NT.
♣ K 8 5   Your most natural lead if no suits had been mention-
                 ed, and even though you wouldn't care for it much,

would be the ♡4. Now, however, hearts have been bid on your right, so this lead is put right out of court even if you hadn't already decided on a short-suit diamond, as you are still more reluctant to lead away from your black kings. Now, with hearts bid on your right and diamonds on your left, you are still just as reluctant to lead a black suit and know you mustn't touch hearts. This leaves you with diamonds, which at least will be through dummy's strength. It may not do you a great deal of good, but it is unlikely to do you harm.

S.	N.
1♣	1♦
2♠	3♦
3NT	

♠ K 9 5 2
♡ Q 4 3 2
♦ 9
♣ J 9 5 3

What would you lead this time? Well, it's quite clear that declarer on your right has a strong hand and that his partner is probably weak except for a straggly diamond suit. A lead of either black suit will probably be straight into declarer's holding, and a lead from your unsupported ♡Q is equally unattractive, as declarer is pretty certain to have a good heart stop. Also, on this bidding, he's likely to be short of diamonds, which all adds up to the fact that your partner should have a reasonable holding in the suit. Lead your ♦9, even though it is a singleton.

Although it is generally unwise to attack in the suit bid by declarer, there is by no means any golden rule against it. Some players have a particular flair for bidding a suit they haven't got and then ending up in a no-trump contract which they make because a lead of that suit has been made to sound unattractive. This is known as a lead-inhibiting bid, and only experience, observation, and possibly a knowledge of your opponents' bidding habits will help you here, and even the greatest experts can be "had" at times! If, however, you hold a solid sequence which will do nothing to help declarer to set up his suit even if it's a genuine one, rather

♠ Q 10 8 2
♡ Q J 10 9 5
♦ 7 3
♣ 8 2

than a tenace which you hope will ultimately be led through to you, then don't be deterred. Here, for example, don't let a heart bid by your right-hand opponent put you off leading a heart from this hand—the ♡Q, of course. Change it just a little, though, giving yourself a heart tenace instead

♠ Q 10 8 2
♡ K J 9 5 4
♦ 7 3
♣ 8 2

of a solid sequence, and now a heart lead is pretty certain to give away a trick. No one cares for a fourth best such as the ♠2 from a suit like this, so you just have to fall back on the lead of the top of one of your minor suit doubletons.

The situation is different again when the opening bid on your right has been made in one of the minors, particularly clubs. 1♣ is frequently used as a "prepared" opening (and 1♦ to a lesser extent), in order to provide for an honest rebid, so if a minor suit

♠ 9 4
♡ K 8 5
◇ A 7 6
♣ K J 9 7 2

S.   N.
1♣ —1◇
2NT—3NT

opening lead would be normal and ordinary, make regardless. Here, for instance, it would be tragic if your natural club lead were inhibited. If partner comes up with any single honour card in it, even the ♣10, there is an excellent chance of setting up three club tricks which, with the ◇A and possibly ♡K, will deafeat 3 N.T.

b.) Attacking or Waiting?

♠ K 9 7 6
♡ A J 7 2
◇ 8 7 6
♣ 9 2

S.   N.
1♣ —2◇
2NT—3NT

Sometimes you must, whether you like it or not, attack early even from an unpromising suit. Given a free hand and no suits bid against you, you would almost certainly choose a short suit diamond lead from this hand. But on this strong bidding declarer is morally certain to canter home with nine tricks or more if you make a passive lead. Your only chance, therefore, is to make an attacking lead. The ♠6 is your best choice—if partner has either the ♠A or the ♠Q you will be happy, and your hearts should live to fight another day. Change the bidding, though, whilst leaving yourself the same hand. This sequence doesn't sound cast-iron like the previous one. In fact it all sounds rather reluctant, and making 3 N.T. may be a pretty close thing. Don't risk presenting declarer with a possible free trick in either of the majors, and remember too that his club bid may well have been "prepared". Play safe and lead the ♣9.

1♣ —1◇
1NT—2NT
3NT

♠ K J 8 6 4
♡ A 9 4
◇ 7 6
♣ J 8 3

N.   S.
      No
1♡ —1♠
2♡ —2NT
3NT

This bidding sounds as though South, not strong enough to make an opening bid, has about 11 points, and may well have trouble with his contract unless aided by the defence. If he hadn't bid 1♠ your normal lead would have been the ♠6, but now don't give him any help in this suit. Nor can you consider aiding and abetting him by leading a heart, so you are left to decide between the minors. The diamond is less likely to give away a trick than the club, so lead the ◇7.

c.) The 2♣ Fit-Finding Bid:

It is vitally important from the defenders' point of view to garner any possible information which may be given during the auction by responder's use of the 2♣ fit-finding bid. So if you listen intelligently you may learn enough to pin-point your best opening lead.

1NT—2♣	Suppose this had been the bidding—let's interpret
2♠ —2NT	each in turn:—
3NT	

1 N.T.   "I have got 12-14 points in a reasonably balanced hand."

2♣   "Does this include a four-card major suit?"

2♠   "Yes, I have four spades but not four hearts."

2NT   "In that case we have no major suit fit, but I could have raised to 2 N.T. in the first place."

3NT   "I have better than the minimum of 12 points, so with your help hope to make a game."

Translated into words like this, it is amazing how revealing such a sequence can be. Even at this point you know that declarer has at least four hearts and not *more* than three spades, and immediately dummy goes down you will know even more, which you may be able to use to great advantage during your defence of the hand. Similarly, of course, had declarer's rebid been 2◇ instead of 2♠, you would already know that he had at best six cards between the two majors. Such knowledge can often be quite vital, as it can be used to determine your best line of attack.

♠ A J 8 5 2
♡ Q J 8 5 2
◇ 7 2
♣ 8

We'll assume, however, that opener's response to 2♣ was 2♡ and that you are subsequently on lead against 3 N.T. Had no suits been bid on the way you would have led your ♡5, but now you know that declarer has at least four hearts, and you are liable to do him more damage if you keep your holding intact than if you lead the suit. It is also pretty safe to assume that your left hand opponent, who bid 2♣, was interested in the chance of finding a spade fit. If, therefore, he has a minimum of four spades and declarer has three (possibly, of course, two), that doesn't leave many spades for your partner, so a lead from this suit too is unlikely to do more than help declarer to a free trick. Be warned, therefore, and make the short suit lead of the ◇7. This is little more than a choice of evils between your minors, but a singleton lead, unless clearly indicated, is generally pretty dicey against a no-trump contract, so your choice falls almost automatically on the diamond.

3).   WHEN YOUR SIDE HAS BID

It quite often happens that your opponents will reach a no-trump contract in spite of a suit bid by you or your partner, or even by both of you. If only you yourself have bid, you will have to decide whether or not to attack in your suit. If only your partner has bid, you must decide whether or not to lead his suit. If both of you have bid different suits you must decide whether to lead his suit or your own. When you've reached this decision, then you will have to decide which card in the suit you will lead.

a.) **Leading Your Own Bid Suit:** The problem we are now trying to solve is whether, having shown a suit in the course of the auction in spite of which you find yourself on lead against a no-trump contract, you should lead your suit. The answer is yes only if your suit is solid or nearly solid. If it isn't, wait for your partner to get in and lead it to you unless you are so confident of your side entries that you can afford to attack in it at once.

N.
♡ K 8 7

W. (You)   E.
♡ A J 10 6 4   ♡ 9 5

S.
♡ Q 3 2

Particularly if the opposing 3 N.T. contract has been reached by way of a directional asking bid, from which you will guess that the missing heart honours are divided, it is usually best to refrain from leading this suit. Whichever card you lead will enable declarer to win two heart tricks whereas, left to himself, or if East leads it, he can make only one. (It goes without saying that, unless at the critical moment you need only one heart trick to defeat the contract, you would duck East's lead of the ♡9 if South plays low.)

If, on the other hand, your suit is nearly solid, there is nothing to be gained and everything to be lost by waiting. Holding, for example, K-Q-J-x-x and a probable outside entry, keep the "tempo" for your side with the attacking lead of the king. Your partner's play to this trick, plus a view of dummy, will give you a clue as to whether to continue the suit or to look for a switch if the king is allowed to win, as it well may be.

As for which card to lead when you decide to attack in your own bid suit, you will either lead your fourth best or, with one of the honour combinations, the appropriate card as set out in the table of standard leads on p. 78.

b.) **Leading Partner's Bid Suit:** Next we come to the situation when partner has bid a suit and been overcalled in no-trumps. Here it is not a golden rule that you should lead his suit, though let us say at once that, if you don't, and the lead would have defeated the contract, you will have a highly disgruntled partner to contend with! It is wiser, therefore, if in any possible doubt, or unless you have a very adequate alibi by way of a better suit of your own, to plump for a lead of partner's suit even though you have no better than a doubleton or even a singleton in it. If you have a good solid suit of your own which is clearly worth setting up, plus a side-entry so that you can enjoy the fruits of your labours, then you are technically free to use your own judgement. For the sake of your subsequent partnership harmony, however, let your reasons for not leading partner's bid suit, and your alibi, both be good!

♠ 5 4 3 2
♡ 6
◊ 7 6 4 3
♣ 8 6 3 2

With a worthless hand lead partner's bid suit regardless. If he has bid hearts at any stage, lead the ♡6 even though it's a singleton. After all, you have nothing whatsoever in mind which could possibly be more profitable.

If partner has opened 1♣, which might be a "prepared" opening, don't lead a singleton if you have something better. On a hand such

♠ Q J 10 7 6
♡ 8 7 5 3
◊ 8 4 2
♣ 3

as this, for example, you may be excused from leading a singleton club to his bid suit when the opponents have gone into no-trumps. Your partner may well have a no-trump type hand himself which was too strong for this opening bid. Lead your ♠Q

which could turn out to be more helpful.

♠ 7 5 4
♡ 8 6
◊ 9 5 2
♣ J 9 7 5 3

With a doubleton holding in partner's bid suit the decision is a little more difficult, but a lead from a weak five-card suit in an otherwise poor hand is no alibi. Here, if partner has bid hearts, don't refuse to lead this suit in favour of your miserable

fourth-best club. Lead a heart anyway.

♠ Q J 10 7 6
♡ Q 7 3
◊ 7 3 2
♣ 8 6

Again partner has bid a heart. On no account should you fiddle about with your spade suit. Lead your ♡3, hoping the suit is divided, something like the last example on p. 35, which brings us to our next item.

Once you've decided to lead your partner's bid suit, you must then lead the correct card from it, and here you will find that the rules differ from those which you will learn to apply in the defence of suit contracts.

From three worthless cards lead the top one. From a worthless doubleton or a doubleton-honour such as A-x, K-x or Q-x, again lead the top. From any three cards headed by an honour, lead the *lowest*, and from any combination of four or more cards headed by a single honour or a tenace, lead the fourth best. With two or more adjacent honours, whether from a two, three, or four-card holding, lead the top. Remember that your aim is to assist your partner to establish the suit he has bid, in which you must assume that he has some reasonable length or strength, and that you will help him in this if he is able to work out from your lead what sort of holding this is.

It is, perhaps, worth repeating that there is a fallacy, more current in America than in this country, that the correct lead from three small cards of partner's suit is the lowest. Here is a hand which was sent to me by the previous Editor of "Bridge Magazine", Eric

N.
♡ J

W.   E.
♡ 7 5 3   ♡ A Q 8 6 2

S.
♡ K 10 9 4

Milnes, which demonstrates how wrong this can be. South was in 3 N.T. after East had bid hearts, and West led the ♡3. East won with the ♡A and, hopeful that West held the ♡10, returned the ♡6 which gave the declarer his ninth trick. This could not have happened had West led the ♡7, which East could not have misunderstood.

Here is a list of just some of your possible holdings in partner's bid suit, with the correct card to lead in heavy type.

A-x: K-x: Q-x: J-x: 8-x: 8-x-x: K-Q-x: K-x-x: K-J-x:
A-x-x: Q-x-x: J-x-x: A-x-x-x: K-x-x-x: Q-x-x-x:
J-x-x-x: 8-x-x-x: 8-x-x-x-x: Q-J-x-x: K-Q-x-x: J-10-x-x:
K-J-x-x

The correct choice of lead from these or other similar combinations will help your partner to judge your holding in it and how best, therefore, to go about establishing it. We will, however, spare a few lines to examine the reason for leading *low* from three to an honour of partner's suit when it is quite wrong to lead low from three worthless cards.

When you hold three to an honour of partner's suit, such as A-x-x, K-x-x, or even 10-x-x, you should forget the old "highest of partner's suit". The basic fact to remember is that aces are best used to kill kings, kings to kill queens, and so on down the scale. So if you happily shell out a top card at Trick 1, it will kill nothing but three other small cards, and its purpose as a fighting weapon will have been lost for ever. Look at a few examples, assuming that your partner, at some stage in the auction, bid hearts over which South has gone into no-trumps. South, therefore, can be expected to hold a guard in hearts.

N.
♡ 8 2

W.   E.
♡ Q 7 4   ♡ A 10 9 5 3

S.
♡ K J 6

If you lead the ♡Q nothing can prevent South from coming to two heart tricks. If, on the other hand, you lead low, the ♡4, East will win with the ♡A and, when he returns a small one, this will be *through* South's remaining ♡K-J towards your ♡Q-7.

```
        N.
        ♡ 6
W.              E.
♡ J 7 4         ♡ A Q 9 8 3
        S.
        ♡ K 10 5 2
```

In this second example, if you part with your ♡J on the initial lead declarer will surely come to two heart tricks if and when your side is forced to lead the suit again. If you lead your ♡4 there is no risk of his coming to more than one heart trick.

```
        N.
        ♡ 8 2
W.              E.
♡ A 7 4         ♡ J 10 9 5 3
        S.
        K Q 6
```

In this last example, if you lead your ♡A, both South's king and queen are immediately established for two good tricks. If you lead your ♡4, whether he elects to duck on the first round or not, he can only make one heart trick. If he wins with the ♡Q your ♡A-7 will be sitting over his remaining ♡K-6, waiting for the kill.

A possible exception to this rule of leading low from three to an honour of partner's bid suit is if the bidding has indicated that a guard in it is held by your left-hand opponent. In these days of

```
S.    W.    N.    E.
1NT — 2♣    2♡
— —   2NT —
3NT
```

light no-trump openings such an auction is by no means impossible. Clearly North was hopeful of a spade contract and East, your partner, decided to stick his neck out (because South might have good hearts at this stage!) by bidding 2♡, either merely as obstruction or to indicate a good lead to you. Lead the ♡Q, which

```
        N.
        ♡ K 10 6
W.              E.
♡ Q 5 4         ♡ A J 9 7 2
        S.
        ♡ 8 3
```

will help him to get the clearing of his his suit under way. If by any chance you are able to gain the lead again later in the play, North's guard will have faded to nothing. Note, by the way, that if you had four hearts in this position (unlikely!) you should lead your fourth best, not the queen, to give East an accurate count on the suit. From the bidding it will be quite obvious to him that this is not a singleton.

c.) **Leading Your Suit or Partner's?** When both you and your partner have bid suits during the course of the auction, and your opponents have ended in a no-trump contract in spite of both of you, you will have to decide whether to attack in your own suit or your partner's. If in doubt, lead *partner's* suit, for which there are two good reasons.

Firstly, it is generally technically better to lead *up* to a suit in which strength is expected, rather than away from it. Leading partner's suit should, with any luck, be up to strength, whereas leading your own may well be away from strength. Only if your own suit is nearly solid and your chances of clearing it and gaining the lead again later, once it is established, are good, may the scales be tipped in favour of a lead of your suit rather than his.

Secondly, psychologically, you are liable to keep your partner's confidence if you lead his suit rather than your own. Your halo will be sadly dimmed if you lead your's when his would have defeated the contract, and it will shine more brightly if you submerge your own feelings and lead his suit, even though a lead of your's might have proved more profitable in the long run. Don't allow this factor to influence an obvious choice, but in cases of doubt, forget it at your peril, as it really is most important.

Other possible considerations are whether or not your partner's suit bid is an opening one or an overcall. The former may have been showing general strength, whilst the latter may have come well and truly under the heading of neck-sticking-out in order to suggest a lead. In such a case he is even less likely to be pleased if you ignore his request in favour of something which produces little or no gain for your side.

Let's spare a moment to consider a few more of the pros and cons for your choice of lead. If, for instance, the opposition has bid strongly and firmly in no-trumps over him, you may be excused from leading his suit providing you have an obviously better idea. Even so, you must judge your moment. Declarer may have bid his no-trump contract on a single guard in your partner's suit if he expects to be able to run off a long (probably minor) suit. If your lead takes out your partner's only sure entry instead of declarer's only sure stop, there may be fireworks! On the other hand, even if there is an alibi for you in this sort of situation, there is none if their final no-trump contract appears to be a rather reluctant effort to play in game when no suit fit has been found. In this case you must attack in what may well be their weakest spot, your partner's bid suit. If you have only a singleton of it in an otherwise reasonably good hand, and a suit of your own, this can be an excellent alibi, though you will still have to be prepared to face partner's wrath if he needs but one round to clear his suit and, once again, your other lead removes his only possible entry card, as quite frequently happens.

♠ K Q J 9 7
♡ K 8 3
♢ 7 4 3
♣ 9 6

Your partner has bid hearts and you have bid spades. Your spade suit is within one trick of being established and your ♡K has more than an odds-on chance of providing you with an entry. Lead the ♠K, which will most probably be allowed to hold the trick, after which a view of dummy and the other cards played to this trick (not to mention your partner's expression!) may give you an excellent idea as to whether to continue with spades or switch to his hearts immediately.

4). WHEN YOUR PARTNER HAS DOUBLED

a.) When Partner Doubles A Side Suit: When your partner has doubled one of the suits bid by the opponents on their way to a no-trump contract, and if the double were of the "business" variety, this must immediately suggest to you that your partner wants a lead of the suit he doubled. Two possible situations come to mind.

S.	W.	N.	E.
1NT	—	3♡	Dbl
3NT	—	—	—

In the first sequence, when East doubles 3♡, he is clearly interested in a heart lead, possibly because he holds something like ♡K-J-10-x over North's suit. South may turn out to have been ill-advised to remove 3♡ doubled to 3 N.T., but this is not your affair. Lead a heart, as your partner has asked you to do.

S.	W.	N.	E.
1NT	—	2♣	Dbl
2♡	—	2NT	—
3NT	—	—	—

The second, and more probable occasion, would be when East has doubled a suit which has been bid conventionally by North. Here North's 2♣ was the conventional fit-finding bid and, when the spade fit North probably hoped for failed to materialise, the final contract has become 3 N.T. East's double of 2♣ on the way is asking urgently for a club lead which, as you can see, is probably the only way to defeat the contract. If East gets a club lead *before* his ♠A is knocked out, he's well on the way to establishing the setting trick.

East:
♠ A 6 4
♡ 9 3 2
◇ 7 4
♣ K Q J 9 6

b.) When Partner Doubles After Bidding: The traditional meaning of the double is that partner's suit should be led at all costs, your only alibi being that you haven't got a card in his suit! Nowadays, however, it is more usual to use a conventional "Watson" double.

S.	W.	N.	E.
			1♣
1◇	No	1♡	No
2NT	No	3NT	Dbl

In this auction the double tells West to lead something other than East's bid suit, clubs and, on the bidding shown, the required lead is most likely to be a spade. We all know that with equal length in the two black suits East would have opened in clubs so, apart from spades being the unbid suit, this is where West's choice should fall. Probably East has opened on a crumby club suit such as five to the ♣Q, five spades to the ♠K-Q-J, and an outside ace. So a club lead would allow declarer to run off his nine tricks virtually unhampered, whilst a spade lead would have spelled his doom. The logic of this double is that without it West would, in any case, probably have led partner's bid suit, so the double warns him to try something different.

c.) When Partner Doubles After Your Bid: The situation is different if you, who will be making the opening lead, have bid a suit during the auction, and your partner doubles the final no-trump contract. In this case his double confirms that you should lead your suit. On this hand you open 1♡ and your partner, who has not spoken until this point, doubles South's final 3 N.T. contract. Without the double your heart tenace would make a heart lead unattractive on the bidding, and you would settle for the ♠K. With the double you should lead the ♡6. East probably has just what you won't be expecting, the guarded ♡Q or ♡A, and he thinks that, as long as he can persuade you to lead a heart, 3 N.T. will be defeated.

♠ K Q J 6
♡ K J 9 6 5
♢ 8 4
♣ A 7

d.) When Partner Doubles After You Have Both Bid: Sometimes both you and your partner will have bid during the course of the auction and then, when partner doubles, it is not so easy to judge which of the two suits you should lead. No conventional meaning covers his double at this point but, lacking an obvious choice of your own suit, it is probably better to lead your partner's, for the same psychological reasons as you will find mentioned in (c) on p. 37.

e.) When Neither Defender Has Bid Until the Double: When neither defender has bid until the final double, this should be taken as a request to lead through the side suit bid by dummy during the course of the auction. This is not an absolute command, though it should only be ignored if you have a good alternative of your own, or if the bidding suggests that dummy's suit is solid. The real point is that it is essential that you should not waste a "tempo" in trying to establish a worthless suit of your own.

However, when the sequence has been in no-trumps only, e.g., 1 N.T. – 3 N.T., it is very different. The double then suggests the possession of an undisclosed self-supporting suit, and the opening leader is expected to try to guess what it is, and, of course, lead it. His best choice will almost always be his own shortest suit.

5). LEADING AGAINST PRE-EMPTIVE OPENINGS

It is not unusual for Acol players to make use of a highly pre-emptive opening bid of 3 N.T., which is likely to be based on a long and solid minor suit with, possibly, little or nothing outside it. Alternatively, the opening may have been a pre-emptive suit bid at the three-level, converted to 3 N.T. by opener's partner. Either way there is likely to be a weakness somewhere, so it is important for the opening leader to hold the first trick in order to see dummy and also partner's reaction to the lead, that is, whether or not he encourages a continuation. Clearly what you are looking for is the suit in which declarer is dangerously short so that you can get your attack in it going before your hand is ruined by discards on his long suit.

♠ A 9 8 5
♡ A Q 7
◇ 8
♣ K J 9 7 5

On lead from this hand when South has opened 3 N.T., don't fall into the trap of a fourth-best club. Clearly South is hoping to go to town on diamonds —what is his weakness? Cash your ♠A and watch to see if partner signals for a continuation of this suit. If he discourages—and unless, of course, something in dummy indicates otherwise—try your ♡A next. The same would apply had you been on lead against an opening 3◇ bid by North which South had converted to 3 N.T. In this case South can be expected to be strong with, probably, a diamond fit, and will be hoping to run off six or seven diamond tricks before you discover his weakest spot. Yes, you might give him an overtrick if he has everything else in the pack and your partner a near Yarborough, but in the event from which this hand was taken South held ♠ K Q J 10: ♡ 8 4: ◇ K J 6: ♣ A Q 10 4: East discouraged a spade continuation whereupon West tried him with the ♡A. This got an enthusiastic "come on" as East had five hearts to the ♡K-J, and the defence ran off the first six tricks.

*   *   *

So much for your opening leads against no-trump contracts. At least you have something fairly concrete to work on and will realise how often it is necessary to forget about the old eternal "fourth best of your longest suit" in the search for something more constructive.

CHAPTER 3

Leads against Suit Contracts

1). GENERAL

THE opening lead against a suit contract, either game or part-score, poses a very different problem from the lead against a no-trump contract. This time declarer will have the power of a trump suit at his command, so the defenders will more usually be cashing, or trying to establish, high card tricks before declarer has cleared the way to cut them down in their prime with his trumps. Against suit contracts, therefore, leads from honour combinations are frequently the best.

Generally speaking, your opponents will have settled for a trump, rather than a no-trump contract, because they are aware of a likely danger-suit. This will probably be one in which they have little, if any, guard, one which the defence could establish and run off against them in no-trumps. Such a danger can usually be eliminated if a trump fit can be found. It can, in fact, well become an added strength, as an ample supply of trumps and a void or singleton in dummy will take care of declarer's own small cards in a side suit, and will kill the trick-taking capacity of the defenders' aces and kings. A good trump suit can be likened to sharp teeth, ready to bite off the heads of apparently winning cards and ready, too, to defend declarer against that weak spot, his unguarded suit.

The defence to trump contracts can, just as against no-trump contracts, be divided into two classes, passive and attacking. The passive, or waiting lead, as we have seen in Chapter 2, is useful when success depends on not giving anything away, but against a trump contract, especially a high one, this approach is far more often doomed to failure. Given enough "tempo", declarer will draw trumps, set up his side suits for discards, and wham!—it will all be over. He'll be spreading his cards and claiming the rest.

Safety must not be completely forgotten, and there will be occasions on which your only sensible course is to make a passive lead. But far more often you will be faced with the urgent need to find an attacking lead whereas, against no-trumps, you could afford to bide your time. Now you fear the power of declarer's teeth.

It may be clear from the bidding that declarer has a fear of his

own—a weakness in one particular suit, in which case you may well
decide to launch your attack in that direction. It may be apparent
that he is relying on winning a number of tricks by ruffing a side-
suit in one or other hand, or by setting up a cross-ruff, in which case
you will probably decide to attack in the trump suit itself. There
are many more occasions than you may realise for a trump lead,
and these you will find dealt with in some detail in Chapter 4. The
most frequent of all positions, however, is when it is clear that your
best course will be to try to cash, or establish, honour tricks for
your side, so let's deal with this first.

2). PROMOTING & PROTECTING HIGH-CARD TRICKS

a.) **Leading From Honour Combinations:**   All things being equal,
that is to say, having no specific reason to avoid leading a particular
suit, or no specific reason for leading any other, such as one bid by
your partner, the card to select from any given honour holding will
be, with very few exceptions, the one shown in the table of standard
leads on p. 78. These leads are used when leading either an unbid
suit, or one bid by yourself, but *not* for one bid by your partner.

Generally your object will be to promote high card tricks and,
as before, the top of a sequence will give you both a safe and an
attacking lead. If you have an ace-king holding, or even an ace-
king-queen, these are good established tricks already, and the only
danger to them is declarer's or dummy's trumps. If you have a
king-queen-knave, a lead of the king will probably knock out declarer's ace, and the queen-knave will become established. With
any luck you will be able to regain the lead to cash them before
declarer has time to establish a side suit for discards—and always
provided, of course, that he can't trump them! Broken sequences
too often provide a good line of attack. If you lead the ace from
A-K-J (telling partner that you have the king as well) you probably
have two tricks in the bag already, and possibly three if your partner
has the queen, or he can get into the lead to come through declarer's
queen at a later stage in the play.

Then again, attack in a long suit or one headed by good honours
may find partner able to signal that he has a shortage so that he can
get in one or more ruffs before declarer can draw his trumps.

There are many possibilities, but before we turn from the general
to the particular, let's compare what constitutes an attacking lead,
that is, which card to lead from a given holding, according to whether
you are defending a trump or a no-trump contract.

On lead against a no-trump contract, you can be dead sure of
winning at least four tricks from a suit headed by A-K-Q-J. Against
a suit contract no such certainty exists, though you may win one or

two, or even three if you are lucky. You might win none at all—a first-round ruff—and certainly to win four would be virtually impossible as, before they were cashed, either declarer or dummy would surely be stepping in smartly with a trump. Against a no-trump contract you would lead the fourth best from a suit such as K-Q-9-7-4, hoping to establish long card tricks. Against a trump contract you would lead the king, hoping to establish at least one trick with the queen. Holding A-K-8-6-3 against a no-trump contract you would lead the 6. Against a trump contract you would try to make sure of two tricks by leading the ace. Finally, holding A-Q-8-6-3, against a no-trump contract you would lead the 6. Against a trump contract you would try to avoid leading this suit at all, in the hope that it would be led through to you at some later stage for two tricks. Remember that you are anticipating shortages either on the table or in declarer's hand and, if you lead a low card, you are going to look extremely foolish if dummy has a singleton and declarer the guarded king or, even more humiliating, declarer has the king-singleton!

b.) **Leading from Unsupported Honours:** We've already discussed the reasons for avoiding a lead *away* from an unsupported honour against a no-trump contract, and exactly the same holds good in defence of a trump contract. There's no such word as "never" though, so the point to concentrate on is not to lead away from an unsupported honour—or a tenace holding—unless you are unable to think of anything more promising. If you feel you are forced to lead from a suit headed by the unsupported ace, lead the ace itself or, as in the case of the A-Q-x-x-x suit above, you may find declarer winning with a singleton king, leaving you without even this one winner in the suit. Don't, if you can possibly avoid it, lead away from an unsupported king, or you may find yourself leading straight into declarer's A-Q or something equally damaging. The same applies to leads away from unsupported queens and knaves, which are equally likely to give away a trick. Remember that aces were born to kill kings, kings were born to kill queens, and so on down the scale, and then have a look at the following examples of reasonably ordinary suit distributions.

1.

```
        N.
        ♠ A 10 7
W.              E.
♠ J 6 4         ♠ Q 8 5 2
        S.
        ♠ K 9 3
```

An opening lead of the ♠4 can be run round to the South hand which will win with either the ♠9 or cover the ♠Q with the ♠K, leaving a finesse position of the ♠A-10 on the table and no loser in the suit, whereas one trick must be lost by him if declarer has to tackle spades himself.

2.   N.
      ♡ A 10 7

W.   E.
♡ Q 6 4   ♡ J 8 5 2

     S.
      ♡ K 9 3

3.   N.
      ♢ A 10 7

W.   E.
♢ Q J 4   ♢ 8 6 5 2

     S.
      ♢ K 9 3

4.   N.
      ♣ A 5

W.   E.
♣ K 4 3 2   ♣ J 10 9 8

     S.
      ♣ Q 7 6

5.   N.
      ♡ Q 5 4

W.   E.
♡ A 6 3   ♡ J 10 9 7

     S.
      ♡ K 8 2

6.   N.
      ♢ J 6 4

W.   E.
♢ K Q 5   ♢ 10 8 3 2 ·

     S.
      ♢ A 9 7

Exactly the same holds good for this combination. If the opening lead is away from the ♡Q, it can be run round to the South hand and declarer will lose no trick in the suit whereas, left to himself, he will inevitably lose to the ♡Q or ♡J.

A lead of the ♢Q from a combination such as this can also cost a trick, as it marks the missing honour. South can win with the ♢K and finesse the ♢10 in dummy for no losers in the suit.

No. 4 is really only a different version of leading into declarer's ace-queen. A low club from West can be run round to the queen, the ♣A in dummy can be cashed, and South's third club ruffed before he draws trumps, which would also hold good if dummy had the ♣Q and declarer the ♣A. But a lead by East of the ♣J later in the play will allow West's ♣K to kill the ♣Q instead of letting him win with it.

If West leads either the ♡A or a small one here, it will mean no more than one heart loser for South, whereas, left to open up the suit himself, or if East leads it and West does not part prematurely with the ♡A (if South plays low on East's ♡J), South can come to only one winner.

On No. 6 it may be necessary to lead the ♢K (one would not hesitate to do so if defending a slam contract) but when you need to develop several tricks to defeat the contract, it is a lead to be avoided. The ♢K will mark the ♢Q with West, and South can win with the ♢A and, later in the play, lead low towards the ♢J for one loser. Left to himself, or with the lead coming twice from East, he will have only one winner.

Lastly, the "Bath Coup" position, an example of which was given in Ch. 1. Give South the ♢J in diagram No. 6, leaving North with three small diamonds instead, and after leading the ◇K, West may be tricked, by a duck from South, into leading up to declarer's remaining ◇A-J, for only one diamond loser instead of two.

Later in the play, of course, a good declarer may be able to execute an "end-play" which forces the defender to open up the suit to declarer's advantage but, as we've said before, at least try to make declarer work for his living!

Faced with a blind decision as to whether to lead from a holding such as K-x-x or Q-x-x originally, it usually pays dividends to settle on the suit headed by the king. The reason for this is that, even though it may be directly into declarer's tenace, the king itself still has a sporting chance of living to fight another day. Here, for example, unless declarer can establish a suit for discards you will make your ♠K anyway whereas, on balance, a queen is less likely to live long enough to score.

```
            N.
          ♠ 9 6 4
W.                   E.
♠ K 8 5            ♠ 10 7 2
            S.
          ♠ A Q J 3
```

```
            N.
          ♡ K 6
W.                   E.
♡ Q 8 5 4         ♡ 10 9 7 3
            S.
          ♡ A J 2
```

Here again, a low lead from the unsupported queen will be, for declarer, just what the doctor ordered, as it will present South with three certain ready-made heart tricks. Left to open up the suit himself, he would either take a finesse into West's hand or, if playing in a suit contract, he would be forced to cash the king and ace and spare a trump for the third.

c.) **Don't Underlead an Ace:** The rule about not leading away from an unsupported honour applies possibly even more strongly when the honour is the ace. As always there will come occasions when you judge that you should break this rule, but it is one you should try to keep. It is the old story of the fact that a trump, not a no-trump contract has been preferred because of a weakness or shortage in some particular suit. If the shortage happens—as it so often does—to be a singleton king in dummy's or declarer's hand, underleading the ace will be the free-est of free gifts for declarer.

As your experience grows, however, you will learn to judge from the bidding coupled with the make-up of your own hand when, from time to time, such a lead may produce dividends. If you have reason to suspect, for instance, that the king may be in dummy, and you have no reason to suspect that declarer has an acute shortage, this may be the moment. The lead of a low card from A-x-x, particularly if it is one which can look to declarer like a fourth best, may well have him guessing wrong. If dummy goes down with

K-J-x, or the king is in dummy and the knave in his own hand, there is a good chance that your partner's queen will make. But avoid this lead from anything longer than a three-card suit, as the risk of losing your ace then becomes greater than your chance of gain. In any case, avoid the lead altogether unless you are sure that your attack must come in this suit.

d.) **Leading From Longer Suits:** We have for the most part been discussing leads from comparatively short suits, three or four cards headed by one honour. For your own comfort, we must point out that leads which are dangerous from a short suit become less dangerous from a longer one. If you have a five-card suit, the eight remaining cards can be divided in a number of different ways, and the third round is almost certain to be trumpable by someone. So although an opening lead from K-Q-x is dangerous for the defence, the king from K-Q-x-x-x is not as dangerous. The king will knock out declarer's ace, the queen, with any luck, will win the second round, and the third round will probably be ruffed—possibly even by your partner. Similarly, fourth best leads from Q-x-x-x-x or J-x-x-x-x are less likely to cost the defence a trick than a low lead from a shorter suit. The lead from a four-card suit is just that much less likely to lose a defensive trick than one from a three-card suit.

♠ Q 8 4
♡ Q 8 4 2
♢ Q 8 4
♣ Q 8 4

On lead against the bidding 1♠—4♠, you have no choice but to lead away from a queen, whether you like it or not. Choose the ♡2 from your four-card suit in preference to a spade or either of your minors. You may find it the wrong choice, but then anything you do on this hand may be wrong. This is merely a good general principle to work to in such circumstances.

Remember that we are still talking about leads in general and not in particular, that is, when no particular suit is indicated, or has become unattractive in the light of the bidding. As in the defence of no-trump contracts, leading away from unsupported honours is to be avoided if possible. Leading away from a tenace is also to be avoided, because of the same danger that it will be giving away a free trick.

e.) **Leading From An Ace-King Suit:** One of the most generally acceptable lines of attack against a suit contract is the ace from a suit headed by the ace-king. (But turn back to Chapter 1 for the variation on this.)

To say that a lead from this combination is always a good one would be a somewhat misleading generalisation. It is unquestionably a good lead on many occasions, particularly on a five-card or longer suit. There is a good chance that the outstanding cards will be so divided that your partner has a doubleton or even a singleton, and will be able to get in an early ruff. It is a less good lead from a four-card suit, though it may well be the best you can find. From A-K-x, though, its only merits are that it allows the opening leader to have a look at dummy, and also to see his partner's play to this trick, before deciding how best to set about establishing the other winners needed to defeat the contract.

♠ J 7 5
♡ A K 7
♢ K Q J 7 2
♣ 9 4

N.
♡ 6 4 3

W.   E.
♡ A K 7   ♡ J 9 8 5

S.
♡ Q 10 2

Again on lead against the bidding 1♠—4♠, you must not even think of cashing one of your top hearts. Lead your ♢K in the hope of establishing one, and even possibly two tricks in the suit before your heart entries are knocked out. Quite apart from this consideration, suppose the remaining hearts are divided as in this diagram. Once you have parted with your ♡A at Trick 1, declarer has only to finesse the ♡10 when he gets in, in order to establish his ♡Q, which he could never do without your help. If you cash both the ♡A-K, he won't even have to work for it!

f.) **Doubleton and Tripleton Leads:** When we were discussing no-trump contracts we decided that, on balance, it was better to select a lead from a worthless three-card suit than from a worthless doubleton. Now, at a suit contract, the position is reversed. If you find yourself with an open choice between the two, by all means lead from the doubleton, as it has the merit of at least giving you the chance of a ruff on the third round.

The correct choice of card from a worthless doubleton is always the higher of the two first (Chapter 1, Section e). The choice from a worthless tripleton was set out in detail in Section (f) of Chapter 1.

An opening lead from a worthless tripleton can never be an attacking one, and is used purely and simply because the hand appears to offer nothing better. This is not so true in the case of a doubleton lead. It depends, of course, on the circumstances, but it is certainly not to be categorically denounced as hopelessly bad, as many players seem to think.

A doubleton led blind merely because it is a doubleton is generally regarded as a bad lead, but at the right moment it can come into its own. It can be used when there is a chance of getting in a third-round ruff, which will be if you have, or suspect your partner has, an early winner in the trump suit. You will, of course, need to hold two or three otherwise worthless trumps, as well as the hope of being able to get your partner in to give you your ruff.

More often, though, a doubleton lead can be used to get you

out of leading something else which appears dangerous, that is, to protect your other holdings in the same way that any passive lead can do.

♠ A Q 7 5
♡ K Q 6
◇ 8 7
♣ Q 9 6 2

Against declarer's heart contract, for instance, we settle for the doubleton diamond by a process of elimination. A trump is out of the question, so is a spade, and a low club away from the unsupported ♣Q is highly unattractive.

Having decided to lead your doubleton you lead, as you know, the ◇8, and when you follow on the next round with the ◇7 you will be completing a peter or echo, showing your partner that you started with precisely two cards in the suit. You may not particularly want to ruff with a card from this excellent trump holding, but

♠ A Q 7 5
♡ K 6 4
◇ 8 7
♣ Q 9 6 2

you were using the lead more to get yourself out of anything worse. In the second diagram you have every hope of making your ♡K anyway, and a ruff with one of the small ones would be more than welcome!

Incidentally, if diamonds had been trumps in either of these hands, the ◇8 would still have been the best opening lead simply because, by the process of elimination, any other lead would be worse.

♠ A Q
♡ K Q 9 6
◇ 8 7
♣ Q J 10 6 4

Here's another example to underline quite a different point, your choice of lead against the bidding 1♡—3♡—4♡, which is influenced by the strength of your trumps. *Don't* lead your ◇8. Obviously you won't consider a spade from the doubleton-tenace, but your trumps are too good, and likely to be too much of a hazard to declarer, for you even to think of using them on possible ruffs. Lead the ♣Q which, though it may not in itself establish a trick for you, may force declarer to shorten his trumps by ruffing and, in any case, preserve your other high cards for a moment when they may do great damage.

The ace followed by a small one from a doubleton holding is popular amongst many players. An ace, as we've said before, was born to kill the king, and though on occasions you will succeed in getting in your ruff, more often than not you will find that your defence would have fared better if you had held onto your control card, either to use it if you need an entry later, or to kill a high honour from declarer's hand. Leads from any doubleton headed by an honour are, in fact, to be avoided except in very special circumstances. If they come off they will be admired by your partner as brilliant. More often they will fail, and you'll have to find yourself an alibi for having made "the only lead to give them the contract.

partner!" You will find more about such situations in Chapter 6.

Finally on the subject of doubleton leads, you will remember from Chapter 1 that the standard lead from a suit headed by the ace-king is the ace, which leaves the king followed by the ace as an unusual one and, in fact, if standard leads are being used, is a conventional indication that you can ruff the third round.

♠ 9 5 4
♡ A K
♢ 9 8 6 3
♣ 10 7 6 4

Defending a 4♠ contract when partner has not bid at all, your only hope seems to be to get in a heart ruff. So lead your ♡K followed by the ♡A and, if your partner *can* win a trick before your three trump teeth have been drawn, you will have found the right line of defence.

g.) Singleton Leads: So far we haven't touched on leading partner's suit because he has not, in any of our examples thus far, bid at all. We are, therefore, still considering blind leads as far as the defenders' partnership is concerned. Now we come to singleton leads, which merit considerable attention.

Is a singleton a good lead? Well, as with so many problems, it all depends . . . One can't make a definite rule, but for guidance bear in mind that the worse your hand the better a singleton lead, and conversely, the better your hand, the worse a singleton lead. A sure trump trick in an otherwise bad hand is a very high inducement towards the lead of a side suit singleton.

Unless, of course, declarer is playing in a sacrifice contract, the better your hand the less chance there is of finding your partner with an entry card to give you your ruff. The quality of your trump holding too must come into the picture. Even if you have K-x only, the king is a certain winner unless the ace is in dummy. In the same way, with Q-x-x, you unguard the queen if you use a small one for a ruff, when she may be a certain winner. But with K-x-x you can afford to spare one, and with A-x-x you can spare two otherwise useless trumps for ruffing if you get the chance.

Holding four trumps, even if these are only small ones—unless the bidding has suggested that declarer's trump suit is long and solid—you should not be looking for ruffs. Your length is more likely than not to be a menace to declarer, and the best attack will probably be to find a suit which forces *him* to ruff. This may bring his trump length down to, or even below yours, with possibly disastrous results to his contract.

♠ 8
♡ A 10 6 4
♢ A K 5
♣ Q J 10 5 2

Against the bidding 1♡—3♡—4♡, don't lead your singleton spade. Your trump holding is too menacing to dissipate on ruffs, and in any case, the chances of getting your partner into the lead to return a spade to you are virtually nil. Lead your

♣Q, which *may* set up a position which forces declarer to ruff, reducing his trumps to the danger line.

Never lead a singleton ace unless you have reasonable hopes of getting your partner into the lead before it is too late to give you your ruff. Without this hope it is better to keep it intact in the expectation that it will fulfil its destiny of killing declarer's king. The lead of a singleton king is even more taboo. This card's destiny is to kill the queen, and kings can so often win on a finesse that they should not be surrendered without a struggle. Nor should a singleton queen or knave be led unless you have some special indication though, from the knave downwards, all singletons are permissible leads in the appropriate circumstances.

Whilst on the subject of singleton leads, let's say at once that a singleton of a suit bid by partner is generally a most attractive lead, though there are exceptions even to this. Here are two very similar hands, on both of which your partner has opened 1♠ and you have doubled the final heart contract for penalties.

	(a)		(b)
♠	6	♠	6
♡	K J 10 7	♡	K J 8 7
◇	K J 8 5	◇	K Q 10 5
♣	K J 8 4	♣	K J 8 4

On hand (a) you can lead your singleton spade quite happily, knowing that your partner will give you a suit preference signal as to your best return lead when you have taken your ruff. Not that you are particularly anxious to ease declarer's life by using your trumps for ruffing, but you are in trouble for a good lead otherwise. On hand (b) your best lead is the ◇K, not the ♠6 which may well cost you a trick in the final analysis. The best laid plans of mice and men . . . but far more often than not you will have plenty of time to make the spade switch and, meanwhile, may set up an extra trick for your side if you gain a "tempo" with a diamond lead.

Another occasion for refusing to lead a singleton is when it is in *declarer's* side suit and you have no hopes of your side winning a quick trump trick to get in a ruff. Not only may the lead tip declarer off as to the distribution of the suit, but it may well give *him* a "tempo" towards establishing it.

A singleton lead can prove effective against a slam contract, particularly if you are lucky enough to find partner with the ace. Here, of course, you would not be bothering much about keeping a guard to a trump honour, and would be glad to use one for ruffing if this would defeat the contract, from *any* trump holding. Here's an example of a quite fantastic hand from an actual event. South's

S. N.
2♡ 3♡
4NT 5◇
6♡

West
♠ 5
♡ K
◇ 65432
♣ 986432

opening bid was an Acol Strong Two and North's single raise showed trump support and at least one ace or void. With eight hearts in his hand, this was enough for South and he bid the slam missing one ace—the ♠A. At tables where West led the singleton ♠5 to the ace which was held by East, the contract was defeated by using the singleton ♡K for a ruff. On any other lead 6♡ was "cold" as declarer, finding four trumps in dummy, did not even have the temptation to finesse for the ♡K!

To complete the picture, here's an example of a "desperation" singleton lead. As neither you nor your partner has bid, declarer's

♠ K86532
♡ 8
◇ 762
♣ 854

contract of 6◇ appears to be unbeatable unless a miracle occurs, your nearest contribution to which it a lead of the ♡8. Lead it with your fingers crossed as long as it isn't straight into declarer's side suit unless, of course, you are hopeful from the bidding that your partner might have the ace.

3). LEADING PARTNER'S SUIT

The problem of whether to lead your own or partner's bid suit, which loomed so heavily in the defence of no-trump contracts, is greatly minimised against a suit contract, and may very well be virtually eliminated as a problem at all. Quite simply, lead partner's bid suit unless you have a very good reason for not doing so.

a.) Exceptions: One good reason for not leading partner's bid suit is if. holding great supporting length in it, in which case you are unlikely to take more than one—just possibly two—tricks in it. Thus a more productive line of attack may well be a different suit, particularly if this looks like being your first and last chance of being on lead.

♠ K876
♡ 6
◇ QJ109
♣ J853

Your partner opened 1♠ and now you are on lead against a heart contract. Take your chance and lead the ◇Q. You'll go down in the annals of your local bridge circle as a genius if you happen to find dummy with the ◇K and your partner with the ◇A! All you will actually have done is to realise that a spade lead is unlikely to defeat the contract and that you've got nothing in your hand you particularly want your partner to lead to you.

If you have a side-suit holding of, perhaps, A-K-J, it is often a good idea to lead the ace at Trick 1 before switching to partner's bid suit. In this way not only will you have shown him how he can get you in if he wants dummy's holding to be led through a second time, but you may well have put a death-wish on the side-suit queen if it is in declarer's hand!

A singleton which you can lead *through* a side suit bid by dummy, if you can expect to take an early trump trick, becomes an excellent lead if partner has bid.

E.	S.	W.	N.
1◇	1♠	2◇	2♡
—	3♡	—	3♠
—	4♠		

West:
♠ K 7 5
♡ 6
◇ Q J 8 7
♣ J 8 7 6 3

With four diamonds facing partner's bid in the suit, you can see that there is unlikely to be more that one defensive diamond trick. An initial heart lead, however, will put you in a position to ruff and you will almost certainly be able to win a trump trick with your ♠K before your third trump is drawn. If your partner has his own ◇A, you will be able to put him on lead to give you your ruff, after which the fourth trick needed to defeat 4♠ may materialise from somewhere. At least there will be no overtrick for declarer!

b.) **Which Card to Lead:** As in the majority of cases, when your partner has bid, you will be leading his suit, it is important to know which card to select. Here quite specific rules apply.

From *any* doubleton, whether headed by an honour or not, lead the top card. This play constitutes the beginning of a peter, or echo, from which your partner may well be able to judge that the best line of defence will be to give you a ruff on the third round. So lead the card in heavy type from any such holding as **A**-x: **K**-x: **Q**-x: **J**-x: **J**-10: **7**-x:

From a worthless tripleton lead the *top* card followed by the *middle* one. That is, from 8-6-4 lead the 8 and play the 6, not the 4, to the second round of the suit, or from the 6-4-2 lead the 6 followed next time by the 4. If declarer has his wits about him and the right cards in his hand, he *may*, by the cards *he* plays, be able to confuse the issue, possibly making your partner believe that the 8 then 6 is from a doubleton, but usually declarer won't have the appropriate cards and partner will be able to judge correctly that you started with a three-card holding. At least it will, as you will see in a moment, give him the assurance that you didn't start with three to the king, queen, or knave.

Don't, by the way, use a MUD lead from three worthless cards of partner's bid suit. These leads (Chapter 1, p. 20) are reserved for leading from a worthless tripleton in an unbid suit.

Holding two or three cards in sequence, lead the top followed, as long as this is expedient, by the middle, that is, the card in heavy type from **Q**-J-x, **10**-9-8 or **9**-8-6. This is no more than following the rule for the top of a worthless tripleton, but, for instance, if your queen fell to the ace in declarer's or dummy's hand, you would not be required to waste your knave on the second round of the suit if partner got in and cashed his king.

Holding three or more cards to an honour in partner's bid suit, lead your *lowest* card unless the honour is the ace. You lead low from the king, queen, knave, or even ten to three or more for exactly the same reasons as when in defence of a no trump contract. When it comes to leading when you hold the ace, with a trump suit against you, you run the same risks as you would do by underleading any ace. This is, of course, the danger that either declarer or dummy has a singleton king, and it is a danger which is even increased when someone else at the table, in this case your partner who has bid the suit, is known to hold length in it.

Some players like to vary these tactics depending on the bidding, leading the honour card *through* any no-trump bid which may have been made by left-hand opponent during the course of the auction (compare the last example in Chapter 2, p. 36). It is generally more profitable, though, to lead low from an honour (except the ace) as, on balance, waiting to play high cards is more productive than disposing of them. Your partner is not likely to have much trouble in judging whether you are leading from a low singleton, a doubleton, or underleading an honour, and can base the next defensive move on this. If he consistently makes the wrong deductions, *your* best course will be to seek another partner!

You should be careful about which card you lead in a suit you have forced your partner to bid by way of, for instance, a take-out double—that is, if you decide to lead it at all. Generally you should hold back from leading the suit unless you have a sound holding. Make, instead, what would be your normal lead on the hand. If you doubt the truth of this, think back to the number of occasions on which, in response to partner's take-out double, you have been forced to bid a dreary little suit headed by the knave or even less and then, as opening leader, seen your partner start off away from his king straight into declarer's ace-queen.

♠ Q J 10 7
♡ A Q 8
◇ 9 7
♣ A J 10 5

On this hand, you correctly doubled the opening diamond bid by your right-hand opponent. Partner responded 1♡ and the contract has gone to 3◇ against you. Don't lead a heart. It is more than probable that declarer has the ♡K under your ♡A-Q, and that your partner's bid was made on a knave or ten high suit. Lead the ♠Q which is your natural lead, and which ·has the added attractions of being unlikely to give anything away whilst preserving your heart tenace for two possible tricks in the suit.

4). CONSIDER THE CONTRACT

Finally, remember that your opening lead may well be conditioned by the level of the contract you are defending. In other words, your lead will not necessarily be the same from the same cards if you are defending a 3♣ instead of a 5♣ contract, or a 2♡ instead of a 4♡ contract.

As you will see in Chapter 5, the defence against slam contracts differs in many respects from the lines set out in the previous pages. In the same way the defence to a high contract such as a minor suit game, which you need only three tricks to defeat, must sometimes differ from a lower contract in the same suit, when you need four, or even more tricks, for success. In the first case, defeating the contract may well depend on the speed of your attack whilst, in the second, it is more likely to depend on developing the necessary tricks.

♠ K Q 7
♡ 7 5 4
♦ Q J 9 8
♣ A K 6

Holding this hand, for example, in defence of a 4♡ contract, and unless the bidding has suggested otherwise, you would lead the ♦Q, hoping that you might subsequently come to two clubs and two spades. In the defence of 5♣ you would lead the ♠K, hoping to set up the ♠Q in addition to your ready-made ♣A-K.

♠ K Q 7
♡ A K 6
♦ Q J 9 8
♣ 7 5 4

Transpose the hearts and clubs in the example above, and in defence of 5♣ you would clearly lead the ♠K. On the same hand though, in defence of a 3♣ contract, you should lead your ♦Q, because you need five tricks to defeat the contract and the diamond gives you the best, if only slender chance of developing these.

♠ A 7 2
♡ 9 7 3
♦ A 8 5
♣ A J 4 3

Against the bidding 1♡—3♡—4♡, which gives you no inhibitions about leading any particular suit, you would not dream of cashing your three aces. You would compromise by leading a trump (see Chapter 4) and hope later to cause the death of one or more of declarer's kings, at the same time as giving trick-taking life to a queen in partner's hand. However, if you were defending 5♦, bid simply 1♦—3♦—5♦, your two side suit aces, if cashed quickly, may do all that is necessary. "Kitchen bridge" may prove the most effective at a moment such as this, but the same hand defending 3♦ should not even consider a quick-cashing defence. 1♦—3♦ passed out would call for the lead of the ♦5, which will give you the power to draw three rounds of trumps if declarer needs to set up ruffs in either of the suits in which you have first round control. (See p. 63, Chapter 4).

When considering, therefore, which card to lead from any particular suit, you should also take into consideration the height of the contract you are defending. Bear in mind that, generally speaking, the higher the contract, the greater the need for speedy attack.

*   *   *

You may have noticed that very little mention has been made as yet of launching your attack in the trump suit itself. This is a more important department of defence than many players realise and we are, therefore, giving it the next chapter to itself.

CHAPTER 4

The Trump Lead

"WHEN in doubt lead trumps!" This is a good old bromide though
not by any means a golden rule. It is true to say, however, that the
attacking power of a trump lead in a number of circumstances is
not fully appreciated by many average and even good players, whilst
the mere idea strikes terror into the hearts of beginners! Further-
more there are good and bad trump leads, so let us say that quite
often you should lead trumps, but only when you are reasonably
confident that this is the correct line of attack in the light of the
bidding and the make-up of your own hand.

1). SOME OF THE "DON'TS"

Before tackling the occasions on which a trump lead is clearly
indicated, let's go over some of the "don'ts". Firstly, unless the
circumstances are exceptional, avoid leading from a doubleton
trump headed by an honour, just as you would avoid such a lead
from any suit at all except as a measure of desperation, as with a
holding such as K-x or Q-x there is always a good chance that
declarer will take a losing finesse into your hand. In the same way,
low from Q-x-x is more likely to give away a trick than to gain one.

Another emphatic "don't" for a trump lead is when you hold a
trump singleton, as more often than not this will be the worst lead
you can find. If any trump strength *is* held by your side, it must be in
your partner's hand, so don't give declarer any help towards a
possible trump finesse with which he may be faced. There's a good
example of this situation given on p. 67 of Chapter 5. So avoid
a singleton trump lead like the plague unless you're in one of the
situations where it is mandatory—see (f) on p. 60 of this chapter—
or unless every possible alternative on the hand looks even worse.

Don't take it upon yourself to lead a trump when another lead is
obligatory on the hand, and don't rush to give up a "tempo" by a
trump lead when you have cause to believe that dummy has a good
suit which you can't stop, and in which you think that declarer is
short, if you have winners of your own in other suits, or think that
your partner may have some. Declarer will be praying for the
chance to discard his losers before you cash your winners. So in

such circumstances you should give up any thought of a trump lead in favour of cashing, or possibly establishing, quick side suit winners for the defence.

Another occasion on which a trump lead is likely to do more harm than good is when you have a good side suit in addition to four or more trumps, whether headed by an honour or not. It isn't so much that you mind parting with a trump, but that you may be able to get far more value out of your trump length if you can play the forcing game—forcing declarer to ruff your, or your partner's side suit, to the point at which he may even lose all control of the hand.

A classic example of this humiliating situation cropped up at the 1968 Richmond Congress. Here is the full deal, (the better the

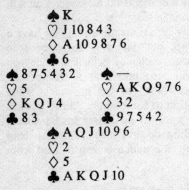

hand, the more it hurts!) At most tables the bidding, with South the dealer, started off with 2♠—No—3♦—3♡, and after North's "positive" response it would have taken a sledge hammer to stop South from bidding the little slam in spades. West players who decided to set up a diamond winner and led the ♦K, handed the contract to declarer on a platter, as he had no problem about drawing trumps and running off his clubs. Clearly here, a heart lead was mandatory, especially when East had stuck his neck out by bidding the suit at the three-level. You may like to examine declarer's plight at your leisure—you will see that, forced by a second heart at Trick 2, the hand falls to pieces.

In very much the same way, if you are the one with a long side suit, whether weak or strong, and have reason to suspect that your partner is the one who is short in this department, don't draw his teeth by a trump lead, as he may well be able to ruff—or over-ruff dummy—when the suit is tackled.

Then again, although there is no rule against leading a trump when the opening bid has been passed all round and becomes the final contract, in other words, when partner has failed to "protect", be very careful before you launch out on a trump attack. It has been argued that fourth hand's *failure* to protect marks him with a good trump holding, but this is not necessarily so. Even if he has, the real point to remember is that your left hand opponent, the one who is going to be dummy, is so weak that he could not respond to an opening bid at all and may well, therefore, have virtually no entry cards via which declarer can get onto the table to finesse against your partner's possible tenace holding in trumps. So all a trump lead will be doing is to give declarer the chance of a "free" finesse.

Don't lead a trump if you hold a singleton in declarer's side suit. You'll only be reducing your own chance of getting a quick one through the slips if declarer needs to cash a couple of rounds before taking a ruff in dummy to establish the suit. In the same way, as we've already said, don't reduce your partner's possible power to do this if you suspect that he is the one with the shortage.

Lastly, don't lead a trump against a slam contract except as a "keep out of possible trouble" or as a desperation measure. You will learn more about these two situations in Chapters 5 and 6.

You will find that there are many occasions on which you have a feeling you ought to lead a trump, but dare not do so because your risk of loss is greater than your chance of gain. But once you get "trump-lead-minded", you will also find that a trump lead often does become the final choice. Now, having looked at some of the "don'ts", let's turn our attention to some of the "do's", always remembering that these will only apply if no better lead presents itself, and if your particular holding doesn't make a trump lead obviously costly. After that we'll decide *which* trump to lead from any particular holding.

2).   WHEN A TRUMP LEAD MAY BE EFFECTIVE

A trump lead, unless there is a strong indication against it, is likely to be effective in the following situations : —

a).   Against a single suit sequence such as 1♠—2♠—4♠ or 1♠—3♠—4♠. In this case the distributional element is likely to be strong, and declarer may well be relying on the control that ruffing power will give him. If you reduce that, you may well do untold damage to an otherwise safe contract.

West	East
♠ 9 8	♠ Q 7 4 2
♡ Q 8 2	♡ A K J 6 2
◇ Q 7 5 4	◇ K 3
♣ K 9 6 3	♣ Q 5

Here, for instance, East opens 1♡ over which you, South, intervene with 1♠, so West bids 2♡ instead of 1 N.T. as he would have done without intervention. This is passed out, and if you look at the two hands together you will see that *any* side suit lead leaves declarer with eight possible winners. A trump lead will effectively eliminate his chance of ruffing a losing spade in dummy, and will defeat the contract.

In this same context, there are quite frequent occasions on which a skilled declarer can. if left to his own devices, play the hand on what is known as a "dummy reversal". This is a matter of using his own trumps for ruffing and later of using dummy's trumps, when his own are exhausted, for drawing those of the opponents. On such occasions, an early trump attack may well spoil his game.

b). Against a high level sacrifice bid, but only when declarer's side appears from the bidding to be lacking a good deal of honour strength.

c). Against a suit game contract reached in spite of one of your opponent's indications during the bidding that a no-trump contract would be acceptable. In a sequence, for instance, such as 1♠—2♠—2NT—4♠, declarer has shown a good no-trump type hand with almost certainly no better than a four-card spade suit, and dummy has shown a maximum raise of 1♠ to 2♠, which must clearly be based on "shape". Two points in favour of a trump lead must strike you here; firstly. it will probably save what may well be a costly side suit lead up to declarer's expected tenace holdings. Secondly, if dummy is hoping that declarer will get home by using trumps in dummy, you may put a spanner in the works if you attack him in that department. Bear in mind also that, on the bidding, trumps are likely to be 4-4, so you can judge pretty accurately from your own holding how many your partner is likely to have. If. for example, you yourself hold two small trumps, you will judge that your partner has three, and will realise that if these include the queen, a trump lead from you will put declarer out of agony if faced with a possible two-way finesse for the queen.

```
        N.
      ♠ K 10 6 2
W.               E.
♠ 7 4          ♠ Q 8 3
        S.
      ♠ A J 9 5
```

Which way is declarer likely to take the spade finesse if you do nothing to help him? The mere fact that you *didn't* lead a trump when it seemed to be indicated, may tip the scales in favour of finessing into *East's* hand! This is just one of the moments which will bring it home to you how much there is to be taken into account before deciding on *any* lead.

d). When responder has done no better than give a reluctant preference to the final trump suit, a trump lead can often pay dividends by shortening what appears to be a short trump holding in dummy. This is a sequence which screams aloud for a trump lead, and here is the full deal concerned. You may personally think that West should have given

West	East
—	1♡
2♣	2♢
3♣	3♢
3♡	4♡

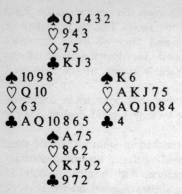

♠ Q J 4 3 2
♡ 9 4 3
◇ 7 5
♣ K J 3

♠ 10 9 8   ♠ K 6
♡ Q 10   ♡ A K J 7 5
◇ 6 3   ◇ A Q 10 8 4
♣ A Q 10 8 6 5   ♣ 4

♠ A 7 5
♡ 8 6 2
◇ K J 9 2
♣ 9 7 2

simple heart preference instead of repeating his clubs, but we are not here to criticise the bidding. What he has clearly done, however, is to show that he has no more than a reluctant preference for hearts as compared with diamonds if, indeed, he has done any more than return declarer to his first bid suit. Particularly with your own strong holding in declarer's side suit, diamonds, it is morally certain that declarer will need to ruff at least two diamonds in dummy. Now as South, on lead against the 4♡ contract, see the difference a trump attack will make! Unless declarer is able to use at least one of dummy's trumps for ruffing, he hasn't even got a play for his contract whereas against the lead of the ♠A and another he will make it! This brings us quite simply to our next situation.

e). When, as in the example above, you have a good holding in declarer's side suit. If he is prevented from—or even hindered in his attempts—to ruff it out by your early trump attack, he may well lose any chance of making his contract. The same would apply, of course, if you had good reason to suppose that your partner had strength in the side suit, which would be because of your own shortage in it (though in this case you may well have to consider whether, by conserving your trumps, you may be able to get in a ruff or so yourself).

f). Another situation where a trump lead is virtually mandatory is when your partner has passed your take-out double of opponent's bid suit. His pass will be based on trump strength so, unless you can see a markedly more promising line of attack, help your partner by making a trump lead.

West
♠ A Q 7 4
♡ 9
◇ K J 10 7
♣ K 10 7 2

S.	W.	N.	E.
1♡	Dbl	—	—
—			

This is the sort of position involved, and your lead should be the trump nine, regardless of the fact that it is a singleton (previously mentioned as being a bad lead). As a footnote to this, remember that East should not have passed the double of 1♡, turning it into a penalty double, unless he were prepared for you to lead a trump.

g). The question of whether or not to lead a trump against a marked two-suiter is a very mixed one, and can really only be answered by a study of any clues available from the bidding. There are, of course, many hands on which, two-suiter or otherwise, a trump lead will avail you nothing, but for the moment let's consider your opening lead from four different hands, each against the following bidding sequence:—

West	East
	1♠
2♣	2♡
3♡	4♡

What are the clues available? First, dummy is likely to have at least five clubs. He will have at least three hearts, and just possibly four (as he was not called on to make an original response to a heart bid, when, with a four-card fit, he would have given the direct raise). He doesn't care for spades as much as for hearts—only a doubleton spade perhaps?—and he has no ambitions towards a no-trump contract, which means little if anything in diamonds. Turning now to East, who has announced a spade-heart two-suiter, he has a minimum of eight, and very probably more cards between these two suits. Either way he is likely to be short in the minors, or to have weakness in that department.

So far as you are concerned, your attack must come either from leading trumps or from looking for diamond tricks, and here you will have to use your judgement, taking into account the make-up of your own hand. Check your holding in what has now become declarer's side suit, spades. If you have more than four cards in it, the probability is that your partner as well as dummy will be short, so your partner will be able to ruff, or over-ruff, as soon as dummy can, and a trump lead would serve no purpose other than to reduce his power to do this. Even if you have three small spades, any missing honours in this side suit will be in your partner's hand, available to finesse, so once again your best attack will come from diamonds. Nor would a holding such as ♠Q-x-x be a good reason for a trump lead. Normally one ruff will be enough to set up such a side suit, and you will almost certainly find that you would have done better to set about establishing diamond winners again. But a holding of ♠A-Q-x or ♠K-J-x constitutes the best possible reason for a trump lead—cut down declarer's power to ruff out his suit and, at the same time, to kill off your honours in it.

Here are the four examples on which, after applying the clues set out, you must make your opening lead against a heart-contract.

♠ 9 8 5
♡ Q 8 4
◇ K Q J
♣ J 10 6 2

On this hand, not only is your trump holding quite unsuitable to lead from, as it is far more likely to give away a trick than to gain one, but you have a perfect attacking lead in the ◇K. Even if you give yourself ♠Q-8-5 and ♡9 8 4, you would have no reason to prefer a trump lead to a diamond.

♠ K J 7
♡ 9 7
◇ K 5 3 2
♣ J 10 6 2

This time a trump lead is imperative, as you may well come to two tricks in spades if declarer is unable to ruff out this suit. This, in fact, would be a moment so marked for a trump lead that you would lead one from a doubleton-knave, three to the knave, or even three to the king.

♠ K J 7 3
♡ J 7 5
◇ A K
♣ J 10 6 2

Now you should cash one of your top diamonds to take a look, before deciding whether to switch to a trump or cash the second diamond quickly. The risk here is that declarer may be able to make a quick discard or two of losing diamonds on top clubs in dummy unless you take your winners early.

♠ 9 5 4 3 2
♡ K
◇ A 8 6
♣ J 10 6 2

This would emphatically *not* be a moment for a trump lead. Your partner is probably as short of spades, if not shorter, than dummy. Take the bull by the horns and lead a spade. If partner can't ruff at Trick 1, you have quite a reasonable chance of getting in with your singleton ♡K to give him another try at which point you would, of course, give a suit preference signal for a diamond return.

h). Finally, as with any other suit, a trump lead can be used to keep you out of trouble when any other lead looks likely to give away a trick. On lead from this hand after the

♠ K J 7 4
♡ 8 6
◇ A Q 7
♣ A 9 4 3

bidding 1♡—Dbl—4♡. it is obvious that you have a good chance of defeating the contract as long as you give nothing away. The one thing you know is that responder's raise following your double has been made on "shape" which, in turn, means side suit shortages on which he hopes declarer will be able to use trumps to advantage. Here you choose a trump lead for two reasons, first, to get you out of trouble, as clearly you don't want to attack from your tenace-headed spades or diamonds, or to release your ♣A so early in the play. Secondly, you want to attack dummy's ruffing power, which you could be well advised to do on a far less star-spangled selection than you actually hold. In fact, cut your hand

♠ K J 7
♡ 8 6 4
◇ 10 9 8
♣ Q 9 4 3

down to something like this, which gives you a choice between leading a diamond or a trump (you would not, of course, have doubled 1♡ this time). and you should settle for a trump lead, on the very reasonable grounds that declarer is likely to try to set up a cross ruff position, which you may be able to frustrate.

You may have felt, after reading the previous pages. that there is, on balance, a lot to be said against an initial trump lead. The truth is that there is a lot more to be said for it than a lot of players suppose, and you would do well to look at any hand with the idea of a possible trump lead in mind before you discard this lead in favour of something else. If you get yourself trump-lead-minded, and as long as you don't fall over backwards into the trap of using it too often, you will find that you may become one of the most feared opponents in your bridge circle!

3). WHICH TRUMP TO LEAD

Having decided that a trump lead is called for on any particular hand, it only remains to decide *which* trump from your particular holding.

We have already seen that it is dangerous to lead a trump from a doubleton honour, as this is far more likely to cost a trick than to gain one unless the bidding has clearly indicated that your partner has a good trump holding—as when he passed your take-out double in Section (f), earlier in this chapter. This could never, of course, apply to the trump ace, which will always win a trick; and from ace-doubleton, when a trump lead is indicated, you should not hesitate to lead the ace so that you can follow with your small one, thus pulling four of your opponent's teeth.

The top of a trump sequence such as K-Q-J, Q-J-10, or J-10-9, makes an ideal lead if you are lucky enough to have such a holding, as it can hardly give anything away. A low one from J-10-x is not likely to cost the defence a trick and, if you feel a trump must be led from a combination such as J-5-3, your best choice will be the middle card, in this case the 5, which may well make it difficult for declarer to read your precise holding in the suit.

A low card from K-x-x is usually an excellent lead, which will probably be no worse than into declarer's A-Q, in which case your king will live to fight another day. Admittedly you might find dummy with A-J-x and declarer with Q-10 etc., but then your king would have been finessable anyway, and you will have got on with the process of shortening dummy's trumps when you felt this to be necessary.

The choice of trump to lead from A-x-x is not as controversial as some people seem to think. If you lead the ace there is always the danger of "crashing" your partner's singleton honour—perhaps even the king. If you lead low and he does happen to have the king, your two tops will score independently, and should he happen to have the K-x, he will win the first trick and continue declarer's downfall by returning his second to your ace, which you can follow with your third. By this time, if declarer and dummy started with four trumps each, they will have only one in either hand left for ruffing purposes, and a 5-3 division will have cleared dummy, even if it leaves declarer with two.

Whether or not you think partner might have the king, it is generally better to lead *low* from A-x-x. Declarer will probably win this first trump trick, but if either you or your partner gets into the lead whilst declarer is working to set up his ruffing position, you will still have the A-x with which to draw two further rounds of trumps, plus a far better chance that partner will have a second trump if he is the one to gain the lead, than that he will have a third trump if you started with your ace.

With an original holding of four trumps, whether headed by an honour or not, you are not very likely to be casting your eyes in the direction of a trump lead, but will be seeking ways of using them to declarer's discomfort later on. If, therefore, a rare occasion crops up when you feel that a trump lead is imperative anyway, make it a deceptive one. Your partner is unlikely to have better than a singleton, if that, but leave declarer to worry it out for himself, particularly if you suspect a 4-4-4-1 trump distribution.

*   *   *

Obviously it is impossible to give a comprehensive list of "do's" and "don'ts", largely because, as you have already learned, your lead is likely to differ according to the height of the contract you are defending as well as the make-up of your hand in conjunction with any light which may have been shed by the bidding. Other possible situations are dealt with in Chapters 5 and 6, after which you will have as complete a picture as it is possible to give.

CHAPTER 5

Leading against a Slam Contract

1). GENERAL

SLAM contract fall roughly into three divisions, sacrifice bids, dead certainties, and those where you think that you have at least a chance of defeating the contract as long as you find the right initial line of attack.

There is not a great deal we need say about the first two divisions. With sacrifice contracts either you or your partner will have doubled, and it will only be a question of how many you can get them down. Your best line of attack will most probably have become clear to you—to cash or set up quick winners or possibly, according to the bidding, you may settle for a trump lead. With the dead certainties you will merely be grateful if the opposition has stopped in a six contract when you are reasonably sure that they can make seven, so you will be concentrating on finding a lead which will keep you out of trouble, with the added hope that something unexpected will crop up to enable you to defeat this devastating contract.

The third division, however, where although you haven't very much hope, you feel there may be a chance of defeating the slam contract, deserves quite a lot of consideration, as there are right and wrong ways of tackling the problem of the opening lead.

Against a little slam there is always a strong temptation to lead an ace if you have one, but more often than not the urge should be resisted. Remember that it takes two tricks to defeat a little slam, and an ace is only one of the two. To cash it can frequently do nothing but make declarer's life easier. Suppose, for example, that he has a side-suit of K-Q-10-x. If you cash the ace of this suit on your opening lead, his king-queen are good without further effort whereas, left to himself, one of his high honours will be killed by your ace, after which he may well have his work cut out not to lose a second trick in the suit.

A good working rule is not to lead an ace unless you have at least the possibility of a second trick in your hand. For example, on lead against 6♡ from a hand such as this, you have a good chance

♠ 5 4 3
♡ Q 7 4
◇ 9 6 5
♣ A 9 4 3

that your ♡Q will be a trick, so lead your ♣A unless the bidding has given you a good reason not to do so.

Some experts say that it is mandatory to lead an ace against a little slam when you have a sure trump winner. This is an excellent rule as far as it goes, but don't carry it to the stage of *only* cashing an ace when you have a possible trump winner. If you do, you may get known for the habit, thus tipping off a wide-awake declarer that he may have a possible trump finesse against you on the table. So carry this rule a stage further and allow yourself to cash an ace if you have some hope, however modest, of a possible trick in your own or partner's hand. Nor must you fail to cash an ace on occasions when you have reason to think from the bidding that either dummy or declarer has a side suit on which any loser in your ace-suit can be parked unless you snatch it quickly.

All in all, as you will have gathered, the opening lead, particularly when you hold an ace, can be a difficult and tricky business. On this next example, for instance, it might be possible to reason

♠ 7 6 4 3
♡ 6
◇ A 8 6 3
♣ 9 8 5 4

that, against 6♡, your partner has a possible trump trick. This constitutes a valid reason for cashing your ◇A, and might even cause declarer to take a trump finesse against you in consequence!

Usually the best chance of defeating a little slam, however slender, is an attacking lead, and lacking any apparent hope of a second trick either from your own or your partner's hand, you should try to set one up before you part with any possible entry card.

♠ 5 3 2
♡ 8 5 2
◇ A 9 4
♣ J 10 8 3

On lead from this hand against the bidding below, on no account must you lead your ◇A. If dummy turns up with a good diamond suit headed by the missing honours and, worst of all, declarer has a diamond void, you will have handed him his contract on a platter. Your best chance of setting up a trick and, at the same time, not actively helping declarer to establish the diamond suit, is to lead the ♣J. Change your hand just a little, as in this next diagram and, against the same bidding your best lead is the ♣7. North's is the hand which forced the slam contract, so you have a good chance that this lead will not be straight into declarer's club tenace and, if dummy should come up with the ♣A-K-J, declarer will probably not dare to

S.	N.
1♡	3◇
3♡	4NT
5♡	6♡

♠ 5 3 2
♡ 8 5 2
◇ A 9 4 3
♣ Q 7 4

risk the finesse so early in the hand, particularly with an ace missing. Choose the ♣7 instead of the ♣4, as this is an occasion when deceiving declarer is more likely to be important than deceiving partner, and you don't want declarer to read you for low-from-an-honour. Let him guess between the possibilities of either a doubleton or a MUD lead.

On a completely worthless hand—an all too possible holding when the opposition has enough of the goodies to bid a slam—a singleton is an attractive lead, particularly if the bidding has suggested that the slam has been bid with one ace missing. Your singleton *may* be facing partner's one ace, which will mean your worries are over. Failing this, he may be able to win an early trump trick so as to give you your ruff before your own trumps are exhausted. Turn back to the examples on p. 51 of Chapter 3, which illustrated two occasions for the choice of a singleton lead against a slam contract.

Earlier in this chapter we did say that you might have settled for a trump lead, but except as a safety measure when up against a grand slam, only very rarely will this be the best choice. Just occasionally you may have a good holding in declarer's side suit, and so may feel it urgent to try to reduce his ruffing power, but more often a trump lead will be your choice because of its being the least likely to give away what may be possible tricks elsewhere in your hand. In other words, although some of the considerations which applied to make you lead a trump against the lower contracts discussed in Chapter 4 may still, to some extent, apply against a slam, the occasions will be far less frequent. We offer you this hand, which occurred in a recent important teams event,

```
♠ 7
♡ J 5
◇ A Q J 10 7 6 3
♣ 10 9 6
```

N.	E.	S.	W.
2♡	—	2♠	3◇
4♣	4◇	4♠	5◇
6♠	All pass.		

and suggest that you might like to work out your own opening lead against the bidding shown before you look at the full deal which follows. What was your choice?

```
            ♠ 9 3
            ♡ A K Q 8 7 3
            ◇ —
            ♣ A J 5 3 2
♠ 7                      ♠ Q 5 4 2
♡ J 5                    ♡ 10 9 4 2
◇ A Q J 10 7 6 3        ◇ K 9 8
♣ 10 9 6                ♣ K 8
            ♠ A K J 10 8 6
            ♡ 6
            ◇ 5 4 2
            ♣ Q 7 4
```

One West player chose the ♠7 which, covered by dummy's ♠9, drew the ♠Q from East. Declarer won, led a heart to the ace and immediately ruffed a low heart. He then drew the rest of the trumps, re-entered dummy via the ♣A, and discarded four losers on the established hearts, simply giving up one trick at the end. The other West, after some thought, led the ♡J, after which declarer was ruined. He got no help over the missing ♠Q, and in any case it was impossible for South to draw trumps leaving himself wide open to three diamond losers if either defender took a trick. In his attempts to wriggle free, he ended three down.

West's decision to lead the side suit was, on this occasion, about as right as any decision could be. But the choice was reasoned, and it is, in fact, a line of attack well worth considering on many occasions.

♠ A 9 7 6 3
♡ J 8
◇ Q 8 4
♣ 7 6 2

S.   N.
1♡ 1♠
3♠ 4♡
6♡ —

Here, for example, you can hardly avoid reasoning that North and South have a four-four spade fit—at the very least four-three, so partner East cannot have better than a singleton and very possibly a void. Unless by some very remote chance he is also void in trumps, a lead of the ♠A followed by another will defeat 6♡ before it gets off the ground!

If you have not already realised it, realise now that what generally constitutes a bad lead against a lower trump contract can be the best possible choice against a slam. On this next hand, against 4♡ you would, according to the bidding, have led either a trump or a spade.

♠ 5 3 2
♡ 8 5 2
◇ A 9 4 3
♣ K Q 4

Against 6♡ you would not hesitate to lead your ♣K in the hope of establishing the one setting trick before your ◇A is knocked out. Refresh your memory too on the hand from the Richmond Congress, given on p. 57 of Chapter 4, when the occasion was definitely one for leading partner's bid suit and *not* the ◇K! But depending on the bidding, of course, a low lead from such holdings as K-x-x, Q-x-x, or even the queen from Q-J-x in an unbid suit, make good attacking leads against a slam contract, though all of them should be avoided against lower contracts.

Against no-trump slam contracts attacking leads are seldom desirable. Unless you have a cast-iron sequence lead, conserve what little strength you have in the hope that the lead will eventually come through to you. Don't risk giving away tricks in an effort to establish a long suit which you will never get in to enjoy; and a hand containing a king or a queen, or perhaps a couple of knaves, should be nursed by making a passive lead.

If you find yourself forced to choose between leading from two suits of equal high card strength, pick the longer one against a no-trump slam. Against a trump slam, however, pick the shorter, as setting up winners in a long suit will avail you nothing if either declarer or dummy can trump the second round, and the longer the suit, the more probable this will be.

2). THE LIGHTNER SLAM DOUBLE

Except when the opposing slam contract is clearly a sacrifice one, a double by the defender who will *not* be making the opening lead, is best used as a conventional request to partner to find an *unusual* lead. Although this convention may preclude a business double of a chancy slam, and the turning of a one-trick defeat from 50 points into 100 (or, if vulnerable, from 100 into 200), you will realise that when two players have enough strength to go on to a slam instead of stopping short at a game, they are unlikely to be *more* than one trick short of their slam contract, so that the defence doesn't stand to gain a great deal from a penalty double. The loss of possible moderate profit from a business double is by no means worth the giving up of chances of great gain from the use of the double as conventional.

The conventional double, known from the name of its originator, the Lightner Double, calls on partner to make the most UNUSUAL lead suggested by the bidding. This means that he must on no account make a passive lead such as a trump, or any obvious lead such as a suit bid during the auction by either the doubler or his partner. In fact the double specifically forbids the lead of a suit bid by either defender, which would be quite normal, and not unusual at all.

Having eliminated these normal leads, the opening leader, doubler's partner, will still have a choice. Frequently difficult to interpret, even by an expert, the task has been made no easier by the introduction of so many artificial systems. However, the opening leader's own hand may possibly point the way. The message of the double having been that the doubler hopes to defeat the slam by getting in an early ruff, the leader will have to decide in which suit this ruff is most likely to be. He should bear in mind that if dummy has bid one or more side suits during the course of the auction, one of these is the likely choice. If declarer has bid a side suit but not dummy, then that side suit will almost certainly be the right choice. If neither declarer nor his partner has bid a side suit, then try an unbid suit.

♠ 9 5 4
♡ A 6
◇ 10 8 5
♣ 10 9 7 6 3

S.	W.	N.	E.
			3♡
3♠	—	4♣	—
4♠	—	6♠	Dbl

This conventional Lightner Double is a valuable defensive weapon, so let's examine a couple of examples of it in use.

You are on lead against this auction, and East's double has specifically ordered you not to lead his bid suit, hearts. So in spite of the fact that you hold his ace, do as he has asked and find the more unusual lead of dummy's side suit, clubs. Doubtless East has a club void—he could hardly be doubling 6♠

without his own ace for any other reason. Which club do you lead? The ♣10, in the hope that both declarer and dummy *may* have at least a singleton heart, in which case your highest club will signal to your partner the need for a heart return, and he *may* then get in a second ruff. After all, this bidding was pretty hit-and-miss!

♠ 9 8 6 2
♡ K Q 9 4 3 2
♢ 7 2
♣ 5

S.	W.	N.	E.
1♣	1♡	2♠	—
3♠	—	4♣	—
4NT	—	5♡	—
6♣	—	—	Dbl

Your normal lead against this bidding would be the ♡K. East's double, however, has instructed you *not* to lead the suit you have bid but to go for dummy's side suit, spades. You may not understand why North-South have elected to play in clubs when they have, apparently, a good major suit fit, but this is not your worry. Do as East has asked, and you will almost certainly find him with a spade void and a side suit ace.

This does not, of course, mean that a defender who will not be on lead must never double a slam contract however certain he is of defeating it—after all, even the masters have been known to bid a grand slam missing the ace of trumps!—but if he does double, he must be prepared for his partner to look for, and to make, an unusual lead. In other words, the double is used to signal the best defence to the slam. Obviously a defender may double if he feels sure of defeating the contract whatever lead he gets, but if he actively wants, and thinks that for success he needs what would be a normal lead, then he must not double.

It is perhaps worth just mentioning that some experts in tournament circles have extended the use of this conventional double to cover game contracts in certain circumstances. But this, for the time being, need not concern you.

3). SUMMARY

To sum up, then, your probable best line of defence against a slam contract will be : —

a) Against either a grand or a little slam in no-trumps, play safe. Keep out of trouble and conserve any little strength you may have by giving nothing away.

b) Against a trump suit grand slam play safe again and, as before, conserve any small assets you may have unless you hold an obviously good attacking lead, even to the extent of opening with something apparently dangerous.

c) Against a trump suit little slam contract, go out of your way to search for an attacking lead.

CHAPTER 6

Deceptive and Desperate Leads

THERE'S nothing whatsoever "standard" or "correct" about the leads discussed in this final chapter. If your mind runs on the straight and narrow path of righteousness, they are not for you. But no dissertation on the subject of opening leads would be complete without at least a few pages on the occasions when you may well find that a completely unorthodox approach gives you the best chance of success. These unorthodox leads may be divided roughly into two classes, deceptive and desperate.

Deceptive leads are designed to confuse declarer when any other line of defence seems hopeless, with the idea of trapping him into taking a wrong "view". Before you make any deceptive lead, however, remember that you may also deceive your partner which, on the face of it, is not at all a good idea. Deceptive leads should, therefore, be kept for occasions when you judge that the risk of upsetting your partner's defence is less than the chance of possible gain from misleading declarer. If a defensive situation seems hopeless though, an unusual approach is justified, and here a deceptive, or untrue lead, can come into its own.

A desperate lead is not quite the same thing, as it may not be deceptive at all. If a situation is desperate it calls for a desperate remedy, and if your judgement tells you that this is your only hope, you choose to take a deliberate risk by making what would, in normal circumstances, be a dangerous lead. You risk giving possible over-tricks on the chance, however slender, that you may find the desperate remedy required to beat the contract.

1). DECEPTIVE LEADS

The standard lead from a Q-J combination would, as you know, be the queen, but particularly against a slam contract it can sometimes be effective to lead the knave from Q-J-doubleton of trumps. If the slam has been correctly and soundly bid this is extremely unlikely to damage your partner's trump holding or to upset his subsequent defence. If the bidding had indicated that your partner might have something in trumps you would not be searching for a means of somehow squeezing a trick out of the suit, but when the auction has sailed happily up to a slam with declarer's trump suit supported on your left and you happen to have Q-J-doubleton, what is there left in the suit for your partner? With no more promising line of defence apparent, the lead of the knave may deceive declarer into thinking that your partner has the queen so that, on the next round, he finesses into your hand. If, when you try this gambit,

N.
♠ K 9 3 2

W.   E.
♠ Q J   ♠ 7 4

S.
♠ A 10 8 6 5

you happen to hit a trump distribution such as this one, declarer may well decide to win with dummy's ♠K and finesse the ♠10 on the next round which is, after all, the percentage play for five tricks in the suit if an honour appears on the first round. Of course, declarer might have played in this way even without your attempted deception, but it is a lead to keep up your sleeve, as it were, for use when you think the moment is ripe.

Similar deceptive leads can, of course, be made in any suit, but it is important to be sure that you won't be putting your partner on the spot instead of declarer, and the lower the contract the more likely is this to happen. This is because in such circumstances partner can be expected to hold some values, and mutual best defence is likely to depend on understanding and co-operation. In

N.
♡ K 9 6 3 2

W.   E.
♡ Q J   ♡ A 7 4

S.
♡ 10 8 5

this diagram, for instance, defending a 4♠ contract, West's normal lead of the ♡Q gives two certain winners plus the chance of a third round ruff for the defence, whereas the "deceptive" ♡J may well leave East guessing and going up with his ♡A even if declarer should duck in dummy.

Holding A-K-x of a side suit against a trump suit contract, from which the normal lead is the ace, declarer can sometimes be fooled by the deceptive lead of the king. If dummy goes down with the queen you switch to a low one and declarer (if you are lucky) may

N.
♦ Q 5 2

W.   E.
♦ A K 6   J 9 4

S.
♦ 10 8 7 3

think that the king was a desperation lead from ♦K-x, and so may not put up his queen. There's an added chance that East might catch on and make life even more difficult for declarer by encouraging with the ♦9 on the ♦K. But remember that there is also a chance that if the ♦Q is concealed in declarer's hand,

East may well not understand and either place West with ♦A-K-doubleton or think that West is trying a short suit lead, miscalculating his defence in consequence.

```
        N.
      ♠ K J 7
 W.            E.
♠ A Q 6       ♠ 3 2
        S.
      ♠ 10 9 8 5 4
```

Here's another combination on which you might bait a similar sort of trap for declarer. After leading the ♠A at Trick 1, continue with the ♠6. Declarer is almost certain to go up with the king this time, leaving your queen the master. Even if he doesn't you've lost nothing, as your queen was finessable anyway and if, when dummy goes down, you find that the king is not in view, you can always switch to another suit in the hope that your queen will win later. The most suitable occasion for a manoeuvre of this sort will be if there is reason to suppose from the bidding that dummy will have honours in the suit; for instance, when North, the dummy-to-be, has opened 1 N.T. and been taken out into 2♠ by South.

Another good deceptive lead can be the fifth best instead of the normal fourth best from a five-card suit when defending a no-trump contract. Particularly if the fifth card is the two, it will mark the leader with no better than a four-card suit, and a good declarer who counts his cards may mismanage an entire hand because of this erroneous information. Similarly, the lead of a third best from a four-card suit can produce an equally good effect, though the danger in either case is that your partner may also be deceived and so will not persevere with the clearing of the suit on the basis that declarer has an impregnable stop in it. Note in passing, however, that deviations from the normal lead procedure must never be carried to the extent of becoming a partnership understanding, for this would be highly unethical. If you hope to deceive declarer, you must always also risk deceiving your partner.

```
        N.
      ♣ A Q 5
 W.            E.
♣ K J 9 6 2   ♣ 7 4 3
        S.
      ♣ 10 8

        N.
      ♦ Q 5 2
 W.            E.
♦ K J 9 6     ♦ A 7 4 2
        S.
      ♦ 10 8
```

On somewhat different lines, here is another situation where a deceptive lead can pay dividends, though in this case it is the result rather than the actual deception which matters. The lead of the knave from a four or five card holding headed by K-J-9 can obviate the loss of a trick when declarer holds 10-doubleton. On this first example, the standard lead of the ♣6 gives declarer three club tricks, whereas the unorthodox ♣J holds him to two. In the second example, the standard ♦6 will give him one trick, whereas the ♦J salvages all four for the defence! Possible occasions for trying this will be when you are sure from the bidding that the major part of your opponents' stop in the suit will be in dummy and not in declarer's hand.

West
♠ K J 9
♡ K J 9 2
◇ Q 10 8
♣ A 9 4

On lead from this hand, think first of what you know. North, who is to be dummy, has at least as good a hand as you have, and his partner was not even good enough to leave in the business double. It is possible, therefore, that your partner has a little something. So what would you lead?

W.	N.	E.	S.
1NT	Dbl	—	2♠
All pass			

All leads look unattractive, so your choice boils down to the least *un*attractive, which is surely a club. But which club?

Should you stick to the rule about not underleading an ace? The double came from North, and there is a reasonable chance that he holds something like ♣K-J-x-x, and a lead of the ♣4 may well look to a reluctant declarer like a low card from the ♣Q. So he may not put up dummy's ♣K and East's ♣Q will win. You never know . . . and even if your gambit fails, it is unlikely to do you very much harm. In the event East held ♣Q-x, won with the queen and returned the "x" to West's ace. East got in a ruff on the third round, which turned out to be the setting trick, so this deceptive lead worked wonders! It was made by a process of elimination as being the least dangerous on the hand, and the only real deception about it was that a good player does not normally underlead an ace against a suit contract, the reasons for which we already know.

West
♠ 9 6 2
♡ J 10 9
◇ K Q J 10 9 7 5
♣ —

Here is an example from match play, where an unorthodox lead was used, not with the idea of deceiving declarer at all, but with the specific object of deceiving partner into winning the trick. If you examine the bidding you will see that the defenders have at best one diamond trick and that, after East's advance sacrifice bid of 5◇, East-West are unlikely to defeat the contract unless West can get in a club ruff. The only chance, therefore, is the deceptive lead of the ◇9 instead of the "correct" ◇K. The ◇9 will give nothing away, but it *will* persuade East to go up with the ◇A if he has it, after which there is a good chance that he will look for a setting trick by returning a club. At the time, the West who led the ◇9 defeated the contract in the hoped-for way, whilst at the other table it was made.

W.	N.	E.	S.
3◇	3NT*	5◇	5♠
6◇	6♠	All pass	

*Strong, for take-out.

2). DESPERATE LEADS

The lead of the ◇9 from the hand above was a purely deceptive one, as it did not risk giving a trick away. Change the diamond suit to ◇A-K-Q-9-5-4-2, and the "desperate" lead, the only chance to get partner in just once, would have been the ◇2, with the prayer that East would be able to win with the ◇J and would read the ◇2 as a suit-preference request for a club return. Notice the difference, because here East would actually be risking the loss of his only possible diamond trick in his gamble for the chance to defeat the contract.

If your nerve is equal to it and your shoulders are broad enough to bear the possible consequences, you may even meet an occasion when you can advantageously underlead an ace against a slam contract! Leading from this hand, for instance, on the face of it you have no hope of defeating 6♠ unless a miracle occurs. Assuming your opponents have bid accurately, North has shown 20-22 points and South (by his jump to 4♠) has invited a slam in spades. Both 5♣ and 5◇ were cue bids and South must be relying on his partner to keep heart losers to not more than one. Your ♡A alone won't defeat the contract but the ♡7, your contribution towards the miracle you feel is needed, might conceivably find dummy with ♡K-J-10. In this case South may well place you with the ♡Q and finesse the knave. Now look at the North-South hands, and you will see that the desperate low heart lead gives the *only* chance of any success. Yes, it risked giving an overtrick but, in the event, faced with the decision at Trick 1, declarer guessed wrongly. He played the ♡10 from dummy which fell to East's ♡Q, and West's ♡A did the damage. This lead might have cost you a "bottom" at M.P. Pairs, but is a fine example of an occasion when, at IMP scoring or rubber bridge, it doesn't cost you much to give declarer a chance to go wrong.

The truly desperate leads are, of course, the ones that risk giving a free gift to declarer, and a "blind" opening lead of the king from K-x is one of these. It can save him from what would be a losing finesse if he holds the ace-queen or, just as costly, if he has these two honours divided between his hand and the table. But at the right moment . . . here, for example, on lead against a 4♡ contract in a team event, one West reasoned that the balance of

♠ 9 6
♡ A 7 5
◇ 7 4 3 2
♣ 8 5 3 2

N.	E.	S.	W.
2NT	—	4♠	—
5♣	—	5◇	—
5♠	—	6♠	

North	South
♠ A J 5 3	♠ K Q 10 7 4 2
♡ K J 10 8	♡ 6 3
◇ K Q 10	◇ A 9
♣ A K	♣ Q 7 6

♠ 10 9 8 6 5 2
♡ 9 8 7
◇ 8 2
♣ K 3

S.	W.	N.	E.
1♡	—	3◇	—
3♡	—	4♡	

power was clearly with North-South, and that if 4♡ were to be defeated East would have to have just the right cards. There seemed (rightly as it turned out) to be little future from a spade, trump, or diamond lead, so West boldly led the ♣K. East's only assets were the ♣A and ◇K, and a club ruff by West produced the setting trick. Of course it risked giving declarer an overtrick but this, as we've pointed out already, is a greater deterrent at M.P. Pairs than it is in a team event, so judge your moment, remembering that it's a thoroughly bad gambling policy to take a risk unless there is a compensating chance of gain.

Try to gauge accurately the field you are playing in. At M.P. Pairs, are you the only player present likely to risk the lead of a king from a doubleton? If so, though you may gain a clear "top", you may equally well gain a clear "bottom". If you know you're doing well, your wisest course is to play "with the field" and make a less enterprising lead which is at least likely to gain you an "average". In a teams event, take into consideration too the strength of the opposing team. Are you going to be fighting for points all the way? When you know the score at half-time is the situation desperate? If it is, you will be justified in doing a bit of gambling if the opportunity presents itself. But if your team is ahead, won't it be better to hang onto the lead you already have by playing safe?

Such stick-your-neck-out leads are beyond the courage of many players, and rightly so, as a high degree of judgement is needed to make the chance of gain worth the possible loss. But if, from time to time, you decide to have a go, be careful not to do it often enough to gain a reputation for it, or the element of surprise will have gone and your chances of loss will be even greater.

Lastly, remember that if such leads work they will gain you the reputation of being a defensive genius, but if they constantly fail they are more likely to result in the loss of all partnership confidence. This in itself is quite a desperate situation, so keep such flights of fancy for moments when you have a strong conviction that you must pull something out of the hat somehow!

Epilogue

BY this time you have probably developed a quite serious attack of lead-itis, feeling that practically every hand is impossible to lead from, and that whatever you finally choose will be the one and only card to give declarer his contract. Don't worry—you will get over it. In any case, many hands will give you no problems at all, as they will contain obvious leads from sequences or from partner's bid suit.

What we are hoping to do is to help to avoid at least some of the hopelessly bad leads that so many players make, through lack of thought and reasoning as well as through lack of knowledge. The knowledge you can get from books, but the reasoning you will have to supply yourself.

If, at first glance, you feel that any lead will be a bad one, try using the valuable process of elimination on the hand. It is, of course, possible that you will still be left guessing, or with an obviously bad lead. You may well find, however, that you have reduced the situation to the obviously least bad, to one which your partner may like, or even to the only lead which can defeat the contract!

Finally, let us make it clear that it will never be possible entirely to eliminate the "luck of the lead". Contract Bridge is not a mathematical science, and even your oppenents' *bad* bidding, which you have no reason to know to be bad, may lead you astray. The "book" lead will let you down. What appeared to be the right moment for a passive lead will turn out to be in the one suit your partner least wanted touched. Avoiding an apparently recklessly dangerous lead may give declarer the one chance he is praying for. One day your luck will be in and your choice will be right, and another day it will be equally wrong. In the sum total, however, luck comes into your choice of opening lead far less frequently than you may have supposed. Once you learn the rules, and when to break them, you will find yourself having to blame that fickle lady less and less, and getting infinitely better results in the process!

Table of Standard Leads

♠♡♣◇ ♠♡♣◇ ♠♡♣◇ ♠♡♣◇ ♠♡♣◇ ♠♡♣◇ ♠♡♣◇ ♠♡♣◇

Holding	Against No Trumps	Against Suit Contract	Holding	Against No Trumps	Against Suit Contracts
A-K-Q-J (or more)	A	A	J 10 8 x (or more)	J	J
A-K-Q-x-x-x*	A	A	J-10-x-x (or more)	x	x
A-K-Q-x-x	K	A	10-9-8	10	10
A-K-Q-x	K	A	10-9-x-x	x	10
A-K-x	K	A	x-x-x	Top followed by middle or Middle followed by Top (MUD)	
A-K	K	K	x-x	Top followed by lower	
A-K-J-10* (or more)	A	A	A-Q-10-9-x**	10	A
A-K-J-x	K	A	A-Q-x-x (or more)	x	A
A-K-J-x-x* (or more)	A	A	A-J-10-x (or more)	J	A
A-K-10-x (or more)	x	A	A-10-9-x (or more)	10	A
A-K-x-x (or more)	x	A	K-J-10-x (or more)	J	J
A-K-10-9-x	10	A	K-10-9-x (or more)	10	10
A-Q-J-x-x	Q	A	Q-10-9-x (or more)	10	10
K-Q-J-x (or more)	K	K	A-x-x	x	A
K-Q-10-x-x	K	K	K-J-x	x	x
K-Q-x-x (or more)	x	K	K-x-x	x	x
Q-J-10-x (or more)	Q	Q	Q-10-x	x	x
Q-J-9-x (or more)	Q	Q	A-J-x	x	A
Q-J-x-x (or more)	x	x	J-x-x	x	x
J-10-9-x (or more)	J	J	K-x-x-x	x	x

*See p. 28, use of Conventional Ace-lead.
**From this point downwards leads from these, or similar tenace-headed combinations or unsupported honours are to be avoided if possible, being more likely to give away a trick than to gain one. Occasionally, however, no sensible alternative can be found, and for this reason they are included in the table.

Where an "x" lead is advocated from a four-card or longer holding, it should normally be the *fourth best*.

Revision Quiz

On each of these hands you are West, making the opening lead against the bidding shown. What suit would you lead, and why?

		S.	W.	N.	E.
1.	♠ A 8 6 3	1♣	—	1♡	—
	♡ K Q 5	1NT	—	3NT	—
	◇ Q 10 9 8 4	—	—		
	♣ 7				
2.	♠ 8 7 6	1♡	—	2◇	—
	♡ 10 4 2	2NT	—	3NT	—
	◇ A K 3	—	—		
	♣ J 10 9 8				
3.	♠ 9 6 3	1NT	—	2NT	—
	♡ J 7	3NT	—	—	—
	◇ A K 8 6 3				
	♣ Q 7 5				
4.	♠ K 7	1♠	—	2♠	—
	♡ A J 6 3	—	—		
	◇ Q 8 5 2				
	♣ 8 6 4				
5.	♠ A 6 5	1♡	—	2♡	—
	♡ J 6 4	—	—		
	◇ K 5 4 3 2				
	♣ Q 8				
6.	♠ A 7	1NT	—	2NT	—
	♡ 8 5	3NT	—	—	—
	◇ K Q J 4				
	♣ J 8 6 5 2				

		S.	W.	N.	E.
7.	♠ A 6 3	1♠	—	2♡	—
	♡ K Q J 10	2NT	—	3NT	—
	◇ 10 9 6 2	—	—		
	♣ 9 8				
8.	♠ A 6 5	1NT	—	3NT	—
	♡ J 6 4	—	—		
	◇ K 5 4 3 2				
	♣ Q 8				
9.	♠ K 7	1NT	—	2NT	—
	♡ J 9 7 5 3	3NT	—	—	—
	◇ 8 6 4				
	♣ A 7 5				
10.	♠ A 9 7 4	1♠	2♡	2NT	—
	♡ K Q J 8 4 3	4♣	—	—	—
	◇ 5				
	♣ J 2				
11.	♠ 10 8 5	1♠	—	2NT	—
	♡ Q J 10 7 4	4♠	—	—	—
	◇ 5				
	♣ J 6 4 2				
12.	♠ 10 8 5	1♠	—	2NT	—
	♡ Q J 10 7 4	3NT	—	—	—
	◇ 5				
	♣ J 6 4 2				
13.	♠ A Q 8 7	1NT	—	2NT	—
	♡ 9 6	3NT	—	—	—
	◇ 9 8 6				
	♣ A Q 7 3				
14.	♣ K Q 8 7 5	1NT	—	2♣	—
	♡ 9 6 5 4	2♡	—	3♡	—
	◇ K 7	4♡	—	—	—
	♣ K 8				

	S.	W.	N.	E.
15. ♠ K 9 6 3	1◇	—	1♡	3♠
♡ J 8 7 5 4 2	4♣	4♠	5◇	—
◇ 7	6◇	—	—	Dbl
♣ 8 5	—	—	—	
16. ♠ K 8 5	1♣	—	2◇	—
♡ 10 9 6 5 3	2NT	—	3NT	—
◇ Q J 10	—	—		
♣ K 7				
17. ♠ A K 6	1♡	Dbl	3♡	—
♡ A 9 3	4♡	Dbl		
◇ K J 9 7				
♣ J 10 7				
18. ♠ J 6 4 2	1◇	—	1♠	—
♡ K J 8 3	2♣	—	3♣	—
◇ Q 8 5	5♣	—	—	—
♣ A 9				
19. ♠ 7 5	1◇	—	1♡	—
♡ J 9 7	1NT	—	—	—
◇ K 10 9 7 3				
♣ K 8 5				
20. ♠ 9 7 4	2NT	—	4NT	—
♡ A Q 8 6 3	6NT			
◇ 8 6				
♣ J 10 5				
21. ♠ K 6	1♡	—	2◇	—
♡ 9 3 2	2♡	—	4♡	—
◇ 9 7 4	—	—		
♣ K Q 10 8 5				
22. ♠ 9 7 4	1NT	—	2NT	—
♡ A Q 8 6 3	3NT	—	—	—
◇ 8 6				
♣ J 10 5				

		S.	W.	N.	E.
23.	♠ K 6	1♡	—	3◇	—
	♡ 9 6 3	3♡	—	4NT	—
	◇ 9 7 4	5♡	—	6♡	—
	♣ K Q 10 8 5	—	—		
24.	♠ 9	2♡	—	4♡	—
	♡ 8 5 4	6♡	—	—	—
	◇ J 10 9 6 2				
	♣ J 9 5 3				
25.	♠ K 7 4	1♡	—	2◇	—
	♡ 8 5 3	3♣	—	4♡	—
	◇ J 8 7 3	5◇	—	5♡	—
	♣ 9 6 2	6♡	—	—	
26.	♠ A 8 4 2	1◇	1♡	1♠	—
	♡ K J 8 7 6	1NT	—	2NT	—
	◇ K 5	3NT	—	—	Dbl
	♣ 8 7	—	—	—	
27.	♠ Q 8 3	1♠	—	2♣	—
	♡ K Q 10 7 5	—	—		
	◇ J 9 3				
	♣ A 6				
28.	♠ 8 7 3			1♣	1◇
	♡ 6	2♠	—	4♣	—
	◇ Q 9 6 4 2	—	—		
	♣ J 10 7 5				
29.	♠ Q	1♠	Dbl	—	—
	♡ A Q J 4	—			
	◇ Q 9 7 3				
	♣ A K 6 5				
30.	♠ K 7 5	2NT	—	4NT	—
	♡ 10 8	6NT	—	—	—
	◇ K 8 6 4 3				
	♣ 10 7 5				

		S.	W.	N.	E.
31.	♠ Q 7 3	1♡	—	2♣	2♠
	♡ 9 7 5 2	—	—	4♡	—
	◇ 10 8 6 3	—	—		
	♣ 10 7				
32.	♠ K 7 4			2NT	—
	♡ 6 5 2	4♣*	—	5♣**	—
	◇ 9 3	7♣	—	—	—
	♣ J 8 6 4 2				
33.	♠ Q 8 4	1NT	—	2♣	—
	♡ K Q 8 7 2	2♣	—	3NT	—
	◇ J 8 4	—	—		
	♣ A 9				
34.	♠ K 3	1♡	—	2♣	—
	♡ 9 5 4	3♡	—	4♡	—
	◇ 10 8 7 6	—	—		
	♣ 9 7 5 3				
35.	♠ 8 6 3	1♡	—	2♣	—
	♡ J 10	2♡	—	4♡	—
	◇ A K 9 5 2	—	—		
	♣ 10 9 8				
36.	♠ 9 7 4				1♡
	♡ J 3 2	1NT	—	2NT	—
	◇ K J 9 7 5	3NT	—	—	Dbl
	♣ 8 4	—	—	—	
37.	♠ 9 7 4	1♡	—	1♠	—
	♡ 8 6 2	2NT	—	3NT	—
	◇ J 3	—	—		
	♣ A Q J 10 4				
38.	♠ 9 3	1♣	—	1♡	—
	♡ 7 6 5	1♠	—	2♠	—
	◇ A K Q 7	4♠	—	—	—
	♣ K J 8 4				

*Gerber request to show aces
**Showing all four aces

		S.	W.	N.	E.
39.	♠ 8 7 5 3			1◇	—
	♡ 8 4	1♡	—	1♠	—
	◇ 8 6 2	3♡	—	4♡	—
	♣ Q J 10 9	6♡	—	—	Dbl
40.	♠ A Q 10 7 4	1◇	1♠	2♣	2♡
	♡ 9 5 2	Dbl	—	3♣	—
	◇ K 10 7	3NT	—	—	Dbl
	♣ 7 6				
41.	♠ 8 5	1♠	Dbl	—	2◇
	♡ K Q J 6	2♠	3◇	3♠	—
	◇ A Q 7	—	—		
	♣ K 10 7 5				
42.	♠ J 6 2	2♣	—	3♠*	—
	♡ K 7 5 4	4NT**	—	5♡***	—
	◇ 8	7♣			
	♣ 8 6 5 3 2				
43.	♠ 7 5 3	1♠	—	2♣	—
	♡ 6	2♡	—	3♠	—
	◇ K Q J 6 4	4♠	—	—	—
	♣ K 8 7 3				
44.	♠ Q J 9	2♠	—	3♠*	—
	♡ 7 3	4NT**	—	5◇	—
	◇ 9 6 4 2	6♠	—	—	—
	♣ A 7 5 4				
45.	♠ Q J 7 5 2	1♣	—	1♠	—
	♡ J 9 8 3	1NT	—	3NT	—
	◇ A 6	—	—		
	♣ 8 7				
46.	♠ 7	1♠	2♡	3◇	—
	♡ K Q J 9 7	3NT	—	—	—
	◇ A 4				
	♣ Q 9 6 5 2				

*Showing trump support and at least one ace or void.
**Blackwood.
***Two aces.

		S.	W.	N.	E.
47.	♠ K J 7 5 4 2	1◇	1♠	2♣	2♡
	♡ K 6	3♣	—	3♡	Dbl
	◇ 8 4 3	3NT	—	—	Dbl
	♣ K 2	—	—	—	
48.	♠ K Q J 6				1♡
	♡ 6	2◇	Dbl	—	—
	◇ K Q 9 5	—			
	♣ A J 10 3				
49.	♠ K Q J 10 6	1◇	1♠	2♣	2♡
	♡ 9 3 2	Dbl	—	3♣	—
	◇ K 10 6	3NT	—	—	Dbl
	♣ 8 3				
50.	♠ K 7 5	1♠	—	2♣	—
	♡ Q 7 4 3	2◇	—	3♠	—
	◇ A J 7	4♠	—	—	—
	♣ Q 8 5				
51.	♠ 7 2	1NT	—	3NT	Dbl
	♡ K 9 3				
	◇ Q J 10 7 6				
	♣ J 5 3				
52.	♠ K 7 4 2				1◇
	♡ Q 6 3 2	1NT	—	3NT	Dbl
	◇ J 7 4				
	♣ 7 5				

Answers to Revision Quiz

1. The ◇10, the top of an internal sequence. If you should find your partner with any one diamond honour you will be on the way to establishing the suit whilst you still have entry cards.

2. The ♣J, top of a sequence in your best suit. You have two certain entries if declarer has to rely in any way on North's diamonds and might also find partner with a club honour or even more, to help you.

3. The ◇6, fourth best of your longest suit, which you may be able to clear with even such slight assistance as the ◇J from partner. Thus you might take four diamond tricks and the ♣Q to defeat the contract.

4. The "MUD" ♣6 or, if you prefer it, the "top of nothing" ♣8. A lead from any other suit would be likely to give away a trick.

5. The ♡6. No other suit offers an attractive lead, and a trump attack, as well as keeping you out of trouble, may well cut declarer's ruffing power. You choose the unrevealing ♡6 as, in addition to giving no information to declarer, it will avoid the possibility of "crashing" a singleton honour from partner's hand on your ♡J.

6. The ◇K. Although this is not your longest suit, it can hardly fail to produce two, if not three tricks for the defence. The clubs, by comparison, are too sketchy and will take a lot of establishing.

7. The ♡K. Don't let North's heart bid deter you from attacking in this suit which must yield three tricks for the defence. These, plus the ♠A and the chance of another trick somewhere along the line give hopes of defeating the contract.

8. The ◇3. The bidding against you has been strong, but your only chance is an attacking rather than a passive lead, in the hope that you may find partner with diamond help before your ♠A is knocked out. Note, by the way, that this is the same hand as No. 5, where your lead against a trump suit contract was quite different.

9. The ♡5. Once again, this is no moment for a passive lead. You have two possible entries in your own hand, so get on with trying to establish winners in your long suit.

10. The ♡K. Don't lead your singleton diamond—your trumps are too good to dissipate on ruffs. A better line of defence is to try to force declarer in your own long suit. Apart from this, if partner is short in hearts, you will be able to win the first round of trumps and give him a ruff. North must have your ♡A but not four-card trump support, or he would have bid 3♠ instead of 2 N.T., so there's room for your partner to hold a doubleton spade.

11. The ◇5. The worse your hand, the more attractive a singleton lead. If partner can win this trick, or get in before your trumps are exhausted, you will at least get in a ruff.

12. The ♡Q. Not that you personally have much hope of defeating 3 N.T., but this top of a sequence won't give anything away and miracles do happen such, for instance, as finding partner with three to the ace or king of hearts and declarer with only a doubleton. Note that this is the same hand as No. 11— quite a different lead against the no-trump contract.

13. The ◇9. Neither of your black suits makes an attractive opening lead so you settle for a short suit. Many players go automatically for a major suit in such circumstances, but you're just as likely to find partner with diamonds as with hearts, and with your three-card suit have a better chance of getting him in if and when they become established.

14. Either the ♡5 or ♡6, attacking what is certainly a four-card trump fit. On the bidding it is highly probable that North also holds spades, so you don't want to touch this suit, and your other kings both lie over the opening no-trump.

15. The ♡2. Your partner tried to pre-empt the opposition out of its best contract, but now that they have gone to a slam he sees good hopes of defeating it provided you make your lead in dummy's side suit, hearts, and *not* in the suit bid by him. Without any doubt he has a heart void, and hopes to get in a first round ruff plus the ♣A. It was a Lightner Double.

16. The ♡5. With two and even three possible entries, this is not a moment for a passive lead. Attack with the fourth best of your longest suit.

17. The ♡3. North will have bid to the upper possible limit over your take-out double, and may well have little more than "shape" and trump support. Attack the ruffing values, leading low so that if partner should gain the lead he may be able to lead another heart to you. In any case you are very likely to gain the lead yourself before declarer can get going on a cross ruff, and will have the ♡A-9 left with which to extract two further rounds of trumps.

18. It may take courage, but the best lead is the ♡3. You have a chance of a trick in the ◇Q and a certain one in the ♣A. If partner has as much as the ♡Q you may establish the setting trick before it is too late.

19. The ♣5. This may possibly help your partner. With both red suits bid against you there seems no future in a diamond or heart lead and even if declarer has the ♣A-Q your king will not be dead. On the other hand, you may strike lucky and find clubs in East's hand.

20. The one thing you *mustn't* lead is a heart, so you have virtually an open choice between the other three suits. Our own choice would be the ♣9 for want of any better. If you count points, there is precious little if anything left for East, so your one and only hope is that declarer will eventually have to play towards the ♡K in his own hand.

21. The ♡3. North has used a delayed game sequence so must be fairly strong. If in desperate straits you might fancy the ♠K, but it seems unlikely that partner will have the ace. If East has any diamond tricks coming they will wait till later, and you don't really want to lead from this club holding. A trump lead will at least attack the ruffing values.

22. The ♡6. This is the same hand as No. 20 when against 6 N.T., a passive lead was clearly indicated. This time against the lower contract of 3 N.T. you can do no better than attack, even though it may not gain you anything.

23. The ♣K. The same hand as No. 21 where, against a 4♡ contract, you decided on a trump lead. Against the slam contract, however, you have no option but to try to establish a club trick.

24. The ♠9. You know from the bidding that North has no first round control, that is, no ace so, as South has made no attempt to bid the Grand Slam, there may be an ace missing. If this should be the ♠A . . . at any rate, what other hope have you of defeating 6♡?

25. The ♠4. It's a long shot, and probably a hopeless one, but if you are going to win a trick at all it is likely to be in spades. Try to take it, or establish it, before it is too late.

26. The ♡7. Your partner's double confirms that he wants you to lead the suit you have bid in spite of the fact that the enemy has gone into no-trumps over it. You will undoubtedly find that East has a heart honour, so that the opponents have no better than a single stop.

27. The ♡K. This is not an honour combination from which you particularly like leading, but no other suit is more attractive. A trump lead from Q-x-x is "out", and you don't really want a ruff even if the ♣A and another found East with the ♣K. Try to establish a heart, which may be the setting trick.

28. The ♡6. You need four tricks to break 4♠ and your best chance is an early ruff. East won't be able to win more than one diamond trick, so a diamond lead would merely lose a defensive tempo.

29. The ♠Q, even though it is a singleton. This is a mandatory lead when partner has converted your take-out double to a business one by passing, which means that he thinks his trumps, plus the values shown by your double, will defeat the contract.

30. A passive lead of either the ♡10 or ♣10—it's a pure guess as to which is the better. All you really know is that you must not lead from either of the suits headed by a king, both of which lie over the opening 2 N.T. bid.

31. The ♠3, that is, low from the honour in your partner's bid suit. He will certainly be able to see from his own hand and the number of spades in dummy that the ♠3 is not a singleton.

32. The ♠4. If the bidding is correct, 4♣ was the "Gerber" request to show aces and North, on your left, has all four. South's spade suit is, therefore, only queen-high, and your ♠K must be finessable. A low spade lead may, therefore, trap declarer into thinking you have a doubleton and East the singleton king, in which case he may go up with dummy's ♠A at trick 1. What other hope have you?

33. The ♡7. Your partner has at the very most 4 points—possibly less. There is a danger after North's use of the 2♣ fit-finding bid that he has a four-card heart suit, but this lead offers your only hope of defeating the contract, virtually all the work of which must come from you.

34. The ♠K. This is a moment for a desperate situation needing a desperate remedy. If you're to defeat 4♡—or even hold declarer to ten tricks—this seems the only possible chance.

35. The ◇A. There's always a chance of finding partner with a doubleton diamond, able to ruff the third round, and he might dredge up another trick from somewhere to defeat the contract.

36. East's is a "Watson" double, warning you not to lead his bid suit, but to try to find his second suit. This is almost certainly clubs, so lead the ♣8.

37. The ♣Q. Your only hope of defeating this contract is to force South to win the first trick with his or dummy's ♣K. After that, if East ever gains the lead, he should be able to return a club to your established suit. There isn't any other hope of defeating 3 N.T.

38. The ♠9. This is a very marked moment for a trump lead so don't make the mistake of cashing your diamonds first. The sooner declarer's ruffing powers in dummy can be eliminated, the sooner you're likely to come into your own with tricks in South's side suit, clubs.

39. The ◇8. Your's not to reason why—your partner's double is of the Lightner variety which, in these circumstances, requests the lead of the first side suit bid by dummy.

40. The ♡9. Both you and your partner have shown suits prior to East's final double, so you have to decide between leading his suit or your's. You certainly don't want to lead a spade at this moment, so settle for his suit.

41. The ♡K. You forced your partner to bid diamonds so you can have no assurance that he has better than four small cards in the suit. This gives you no reason to touch a suit headed by A-Q so, as you have an excellent alternative available, take it.

42. An uninformative middle club. You have no hope of getting in a ruff by leading your singleton so play as safe as you can. Your only hope of a trick is the ♡K.

43. The ◇K. This is not the time for a trump lead or for your singleton heart, which might just tip declarer off that it *is* a singleton. You will probably be able to trump this side suit as soon as dummy can—if not sooner.

44. The ♣A. It is almost a certainty that you will be able to take a trump trick on this hand, so at least try to get the second trick needed from your ace.

45. The ♡3, though this is definitely the best of a bad lot. With both black suits bid against you there is no sense in trying to attack in those suits, and your ◇A would be a very poor alternative.

46. The ♡K, from a suit which might well become established in one round whilst you still have the ◇A for an entry.

47. The ♡K. East has made it crystal clear that he has a genuine heart suit, and will be overjoyed to find you actually have the ♡K! He will lead spades through to you when he gets in. North's 3♡ must have been a directional asking bid, by the way.

48. The ♠K. Your trumps are too good to be dissipated on ruffs, so the best attack will come from establishing one or more spade tricks for your side. Any hearts available will come later—and so will your diamonds, particularly if you are able to force declarer to ruff, which might even "promote" your ◇9.

49. The ♠K. This is another occasion on which both you and your partner have bid during the auction, even though there seem hardly enough points in the pack for all the bidding! You must choose between your suit and partner's, but your spades may well become established in one round and, on the bidding, the ◇K looks like an entry. So this time lead your own suit.

50. The ♠5. Dummy is marked with no better than three trumps and a diamond shortage, so it looks as though declarer will be relying on ruffing power. The sooner this is cut down the better, and this lead isn't likely to give away a spade trick while it runs no risk of giving away a heart if declarer has ♡K-J. You have hopes of making two diamonds, the ♠K, and a fourth trick may come along from partner's hand.

51. The ♠7. East has almost certainly got a long, solid, undisclosed suit and has asked you to try to find it. Your best chance is your shortest suit.

52. The ♣7. Another moment when East has asked you, by his "Watson" double, not to lead his bid suit but to try to find his second suit. This is most likely to be clubs.

Details of other books on bridge published in Unwin Paperbacks are given on the following pages.

Learn Bridge with the Lederers

TONY AND RHODA LEDERER

This book recreates the early teaching under the Lederer methods in 'terms' of ten lessons each. It is intended for absolute beginners, taking them from the basics to the point where they need only experience to become reasonably sound players. The bidding methods followed are the simple ones: simple Acol with a weak No Trump and as few frills as possible presented in the conversational tone which made the Lederers' classroom style so successful. The book can be used by any beginner who may have been daunted by what he has learnt of the game elsewhere.

The ABC of Contract Bridge

BEN COHEN AND RHODA LEDERER

'Ideal for a complete beginner'
Birmingham Post

'Beginners should find this book of great assistance'
The Scotsman

Master Bridge by Question and Answer

ALAN TRUSCOTT

adapted by RHODA and TONY LEDERER

This book allows you to look over the shoulder of an expert player to help you improve your game. There are three main features to *Master Bridge*. First there are mind-stretching quiz questions based on actual hands from major championships. Then the reader can turn to the answers and rate himself according to a point scale of ability in bidding play and overall competence. Finally the actual play of each hand, on which the questions are based, is described in detail demonstrating each problem in a full 52-card setting. Alan Truscott, a former British championship player and European champion, has been Executive Editor of *The Official Encyclopaedia of Bridge*.

Aces and Places

The International Bridge Circuit

RIXI MARKUS

Rixi Markus, long established as one of the world's leading women players, provides a vivid study of how top contracts are made. She describes in detail the bids and play of stars like the Italian Blue Team, the Omar Sharif Circus and other top European and British players. She describes and analyses some 75 hands and any one of them played by an amateur player would be the highlight of their career.

Bid Boldly, Play Safe

RIXI MARKUS

This edition of Rixi Markus' famous first book has been completely revised, and much new material has been added. In it she explains how the cultivation of a logical approach can enable the average player to achieve a high standard of play without memorizing conventions or complicated rules of thumb because it improves his technique, his judgement and his grasp of the game's essential principles.

'There is much in this book to instruct and delight you, and there are many excellent illustrative hands'.

The Financial Times

Bridge-Table Tales

RIXI MARKUS

Rixi Markus has personally collected here hands from celebrated players that are memorable for a variety of reasons. As the title states, each is a bridge-table tale, told in a way that enables us to appreciate the declarers' or defenders' thinking at the table.

All the hands discussed make points that will stimulate the ordinary player to think more clearly, be it at bidding, or card play. 'Making the Defence Help', 'Good Guess Rewarded', 'Forestalling a Squeeze' or 'A Winning Two-down' are typical chapter titles. The making of 'impossible' contracts against all the odds and 'killing leads' are some of the most memorable of these Rixi stories, or, more appropriately, 'tales', coming as they do from a great player already so popular as a bridge writer in the *Guardian*.